An Essential Latin Grammar

An Essential
Latin Grammar

W. MICHAEL WILSON

PRINCIPAL TEACHER OF CLASSICS
ALLOA ACADEMY

MACMILLAN

ST MARTIN'S PRESS

Published by
MACMILLAN AND CO LTD
Little Essex Street London W C2
and also at Bombay Calcutta and Madras
Macmillan South Africa (Publishers) Pty Ltd Johannesburg
The Macmillan Company of Australia Pty Ltd Melbourne
The Macmillan Company of Canada Ltd Toronto
St Martin's Press Inc New York

Printed in Great Britain by
ROBERT MACLEHOSE AND CO LTD
The University Press, Glasgow

Contents

Preface

In this book I have endeavoured to give a skeleton outline of Latin Accidence and Syntax up to 'O' level. Much unnecessary 'lumber' which clutters up the pages of many of our grammars has been omitted. Wherever possible I have avoided using technical terms and have attempted to explain Syntax rules for translating Latin into English rather than for turning English into Latin.

W. M. W.

Essential Accidence

I. NOUNS

1. Latin Nouns are divided into five groups called **Declensions.** Most nouns have **six** cases denoted by varied endings.

2. FIRST DECLENSION
All Nouns of the First Declension end in –**a** in the Nominative Singular.

rēgīna – rēgīnae (f), *queen.*

	SINGULAR	PLURAL
Nom.	rēgīna	rēgīnae
Voc.	rēgīna	rēgīnae
Acc.	rēgīnam	rēgīnās
Gen.	rēgīnae	rēgīnārum
Dat.	rēgīnae	rēgīnīs
Abl.	rēgīnā	rēgīnīs

3. Dea, *goddess* and **fīlia,** *daughter* have their Dative and Ablative Plural, deā**bus** and fīliā**bus.**

4. Most Nouns of the First Declension are **Feminine** except, **poēta,** *poet,* **agricola,** *farmer,* **nauta,** *sailor* and **scrība,** *clerk* which are **Masculine.**

5. SECOND DECLENSION

Masculine Nouns of the Second Declension end in **–us** in the Nominative Singular, apart from a few ending in **–er** or **–r**. Neuter Nouns of the Second Declension end in **–um**.

servus – servī (m), *slave.*   **ager – agrī** (m), *field.*

	SINGULAR	PLURAL	SINGULAR	PLURAL
Nom.	servus	servī	ager	agrī
Voc.	serve	servī	ager	agrī
Acc.	servum	servōs	agrum	agrōs
Gen.	servī	servōrum	agrī	agrōrum
Dat.	servō	servīs	agrō	agrīs
Abl.	servō	servīs	agrō	agrīs

puer – puerī (m), *boy.*   **vir – virī** (m), *man.*

	SINGULAR	PLURAL	SINGULAR	PLURAL
Nom.	puer	puerī	vir	virī
Voc.	puer	puerī	vir	virī
Acc.	puerum	puerōs	virum	virōs
Gen.	puerī	puerōrum	virī	virōrum
Dat.	puerō	puerīs	virō	virīs
Abl.	puerō	puerīs	virō	virīs

bellum – bellī (n), *war.*   **deus – deī** (m), *god.*

	SINGULAR	PLURAL	SINGULAR	PLURAL
Nom.	bellum	bella	deus	dī (deī)
Voc.	bellum	bella	deus	dī (deī)
Acc.	bellum	bella	deum	deōs
Gen.	bellī	bellōrum	deī	deōrum (deum)
Dat.	bellō	bellīs	deō	dīs (deīs)
Abl.	bellō	bellīs	deō	dīs (deīs)

6. (*a*) **Fīlius**, *son* and **Proper** names ending in **–ius**, such as **Cornēlius, Pompēius** have their Vocative Singular in **–ī**.

e.g. fīlī, Cornēlī, Pompēī

(*b*) **Meus-a-um**, *my, mine,* has its Vocative Masculine Singular **mī**.

7. THIRD DECLENSION

The Third Declension is by far the biggest group of Nouns. They may be divided into **Five** groups (i) **Increasing** (ii) **Non-increasing** (iii) **Family Group** (iv) **Monosyllabics with stems ending in two consonants** (v) **Neuters ending in -ĕ, -al, -ar.** All genders are found.

N.B. The stem is found by taking the **Genitive Singular** and cutting off the ending, e.g. legiō, Genitive Singular legiōnis has the stem **legiōn–**

8. *Increasing Nouns*

A Noun is said to increase when it has **more** syllables in its **Genitive Singular** than in its **Nominative Singular.** An Increasing Noun has its Genitive Plural in **–um.**

mīles – mīlitis (m), *soldier.*   **statiō – statiōnis** (f), *outpost.*

	SINGULAR	PLURAL	SINGULAR	PLURAL
Nom.	mīles	mīlitēs	statiō	statiōnēs
Voc.	mīles	mīlitēs	statiō	statiōnēs
Acc.	mīlitem	mīlitēs	statiōnem	statiōnēs
Gen.	mīlitis	mīlitum	statiōnis	statiōnūm
Dat.	mīlitī	mīlitibus	statiōnī	statiōnibus
Abl.	mīlite	mīlitibus	statiōne	statiōnibus

flūmen – flūminis (n), *river.*   **opus – operis** (n), *job, task.*

	SINGULAR	PLURAL	SINGULAR	PLURAL
Nom.	flūmen	flūmina	opus	opera
Voc.	flūmen	flūmina	opus	opera
Acc.	flūmen	flūmina	opus	opera
Gen.	flūminis	flūminum	operis	operum
Dat.	flūminī	flūminibus	operī	operibus
Abl.	flūmine	flūminibus	opere	operibus

9. *Non-Increasing Nouns*

A Non-Increasing Noun has the **same** number of syllables in its **Genitive Singular** as in its **Nominative Singular.** A Non-Increasing Noun has its Genitive Plural in **–ium.**

hostis – hostis (m), *enemy.*   **nāvis – nāvis** (f), *ship.*

	SINGULAR	PLURAL	SINGULAR	PLURAL
Nom.	hostis	hostēs	nāvis	nāvēs
Voc.	hostis	hostēs	nāvis	nāvēs
Acc.	hostem	hostēs	nāvem	nāvēs
Gen.	hostis	hostium	nāvis	nāvium
Dat.	hostī	hostibus	nāvī	nāvibus
Abl.	hoste	hostibus	nāve	nāvibus

10. *Family Group*

The Family Group consists of **six** Nouns which are Non-Increasing but have their Genitive Plural in **–um**.

pater	– patris	(m),	*father*
māter	– mātris	(f),	*mother*
frāter	– frātris	(m),	*brother*
senex	– senis	(m),	*old man*
iuvenis	– iuvenis	(m),	*young man*
canis	– canis	(m),	*dog.*

11. *Monosyllabic Nouns*

Monosyllabic Nouns (i.e. Nouns of **one** syllable in the Nominative Singular) whose stem ends in **two consonants** have their Genitive Plural in **–ium**.

e.g. nox	– noctis	(f),	*night*
mōns	– montis	(m),	*mountain*
pōns	– pontis	(m),	*bridge*
fōns	– fontis	(m),	*fountain*
gēns	– gentis	(f),	*tribe*
urbs	– urbis	(f),	*city*
dēns	– dentis	(m),	*tooth*
os	– ossis	(n),	*bone*
as	– assis	(n),	*as* (a Roman coin)
arx	– arcis	(f),	*citadel*

12. *Neuter Nouns*

Neuter Nouns ending in **–ĕ, –al, –ar** decline as follows.

animal – animālis (n), *animal.*   **mare – maris** (n), *sea.*

	SINGULAR	PLURAL	SINGULAR	PLURAL
Nom.	animal	animālia	mare	maria
Voc.	animal	animālia	mare	maria
Acc.	animal	animālia	mare	maria
Gen.	animālis	animālium	maris	—
Dat.	animālī	animālibus	marī	maribus
Abl.	animālī	animālibus	marī	maribus

also **cubīle – cubīlis** (n), *bed* and **calcar – calcāris** (n), *spur*

13. The following Nouns are irregular in declension.

vīs (f), *force* (in pl., *strength*).   **bōs – bovis** (m), *ox.*

	SINGULAR	PLURAL	SINGULAR	PLURAL
Nom.	vīs	vīrēs	bōs	bovēs
Voc.	vīs	vīrēs	bōs	bovēs
Acc.	vim	vīrēs	bovem	bovēs
Gen.	—	vīrium	bovis	boum
Dat.	—	vīribus	bovī	bōbus (bubus)
Abl.	vī	vīribus	bove	bōbus (bubus)

Iuppiter – Iovis (m), *Jupiter.*

Nom.	Iuppiter	Gen.	Iovis
Voc.	Iuppiter	Dat.	Iovī
Acc.	Iovem	Abl.	Iove

14. FOURTH DECLENSION

Fourth Declension Nouns end in **–us** in the Nominative Singular and are mostly **Masculine.** There are two common **Neuter** Nouns which end in **–u** in the Nominative Singular, **genū-ūs**, *knee* and **cornu-ūs**, *horn, wing of an army.*

magistrātus – magistrātūs (m), *magistrate.*
genū – genūs (n), *knee.*

	SINGULAR	PLURAL	SINGULAR	PLURAL
Nom.	magistrātus	magistrātūs	genū	genua
Voc.	magistrātus	magistrātūs	genū	genua
Acc.	magistrātum	magistrātūs	genū	genua
Gen.	magistrātūs	magistrātuum	genūs	genuum
Dat.	magistrātuī	magistrātibus	genū	genibus
Abl.	magistrātū	magistrātibus	genū	genibus

15. There are a few Feminine Nouns, the commonest of which are, **manus-ūs** (f), *hand*, and **domus-ūs** (f), *house, home*.

	SINGULAR	PLURAL
Nom.	dom**us**	dom**ūs**
Voc.	dom**us**	dom**ūs**
Acc.	dom**um**	dom**ūs** (dom**ōs**)
Gen.	dom**ūs**	dom**uum** (dom**ōrum**)
Dat.	dom**uī**	dom**ibus**
Abl.	dom**ō**	dom**ibus**

16. Fifth Declension

Fifth Declension Nouns end in **–ēs** in the Nominative Singular.

     diēs – diēī (m), *day*.   **rēs – reī** (f), *thing*.

	SINGULAR	PLURAL	SINGULAR	PLURAL
Nom.	di**ēs**	di**ēs**	r**ēs**	r**ēs**
Voc.	di**ēs**	di**ēs**	r**ēs**	r**ēs**
Acc.	di**em**	di**ēs**	r**em**	r**ēs**
Gen.	di**ēī**	di**ērum**	r**eī**	r**ērum**
Dat.	di**ēī**	di**ēbus**	r**eī**	r**ēbus**
Abl.	di**ē**	di**ēbus**	r**ē**	r**ēbus**

II. ADJECTIVES AND ADVERBS

Latin Adjectives can be arranged in **two** groups, those with First and Second Declension endings, and those with Third Declension endings.

17. First and Second Declension Adjectives
     altus-a-um, *high, deep.*

	SINGULAR			PLURAL		
	M	*F*	*N*	*M*	*F*	*N*
Nom.	alt**us**	alt**a**	alt**um**	alt**ī**	alt**ae**	alt**a**
Voc.	alt**e**	alt**a**	alt**um**	alt**ī**	alt**ae**	alt**a**
Acc.	alt**um**	alt**am**	alt**um**	alt**ōs**	alt**ās**	alt**a**
Gen.	alt**ī**	alt**ae**	alt**ī**	alt**ōrum**	alt**ārum**	alt**ōrum**
Dat.	alt**ō**	alt**ae**	alt**ō**	alt**īs**	alt**īs**	alt**īs**
Abl.	alt**ō**	alt**ā**	alt**ō**	alt**īs**	alt**īs**	alt**īs**

miser-misera-miserum, *wretched*.

	SINGULAR			PLURAL		
	M	*F*	*N*	*M*	*F*	*N*
N.	miser	misera	miserum	miserī	miserae	misera
V.	miser	misera	miserum	miserī	miserae	misera
A.	miserum	miseram	miserum	miserōs	miserās	misera
G.	miserī	miserae	miserī	miserōrum	miserārum	miserōrum
D.	miserō	miserae	miserō	miserīs	miserīs	miserīs
A.	miserō	miserā	miserō	miserīs	miserīs	miserīs

Declined like miser, i.e. keep the **e** are,

asper – aspera – asperum, *rough*
līber – lībera – līberum, *free*
tener – tenera – tenerum, *tender*.

niger – nigra – nigrum, *black*.

	SINGULAR			PLURAL		
	M	*F*	*N*	*M*	*F*	*N*
Nom.	niger	nigra	nigrum	nigrī	nigrae	nigra
Voc.	niger	nigra	nigrum	nigrī	nigrae	nigra
Acc.	nigrum	nigram	nigrum	nigrōs	nigrās	nigra
Gen.	nigrī	nigrae	nigrī	nigrōrum	nigrārum	nigrōrum
Dat.	nigrō	nigrae	nigrō	nigrīs	nigrīs	nigrīs
Abl.	nigrō	nigrā	nigrō	nigrīs	nigrīs	nigrīs

Declined like niger, i.e. drop the **e** are,

aeger   – aegra   – aegrum, *sick*
pulcher – pulchra – pulchrum, *beautiful*
crēber – crēbra – crēbrum, *frequent*
piger   – pigra   – pigrum, *lazy*.

18. ūllus – ūlla – ūllum, *any*.

	SINGULAR			PLURAL		
	M	*F*	*N*	*M*	*F*	*N*
Nom.	ūllus	ūlla	ūllum	ūllī	ūllae	ūlla
Acc.	ūllum	ūllam	ūllum	ūllōs	ūllās	ūlla
Gen.	ūllīus	ūllīus	ūllīus	ūllōrum	ūllārum	ūllōrum
Dat.	ūllī	ūllī	ūllī	ūllīs	ūllīs	ūllīs
Abl.	ūllō	ūllā	ūllō	ūllīs	ūllīs	ūllīs

Declined like ūllus are,

nūllus	– a	– um, *no, none*
ūnus	– a	– um, *one*
sōlus	– a	– um, *alone, only*
tōtus	– a	– um, *whole of*
alius	– a	– ud, *another*
uter	– utra	– utrum, *which of two*
uterque	– utraque	– utrumque, *each of two*
neuter	– neutra	– neutrum, *neither of two*
alter	– altera	– alterum, *the one, the other of two.*

19. THIRD DECLENSION ADJECTIVES

(a) Adjectives with **one** ending in the **Nominative Singular**.
ingēns – ingēns – ingēns, *huge.*

	SINGULAR			PLURAL		
	M	*F*	*N*	*M*	*F*	*N*
Nom.	ingēns	ingēns	ingēns	ingentēs	ingentēs	ingentia
Voc.	ingēns	ingēns	ingēns	ingentēs	ingentēs	ingentia
Acc.	ingentem	ingentem	ingēns	ingentēs	ingentēs	ingentia
Gen.	ingentis	ingentis	ingentis	ingentium	ingentium	ingentium
Dat.	ingentī	ingentī	ingentī	ingentibus	ingentibus	ingentibus
Abl.	ingentī	ingentī	ingentī	ingentibus	ingentibus	ingentibus

fēlīx – fēlīx – fēlīx, *happy.*

	SINGULAR			PLURAL		
	M	*F*	*N*	*M*	*F*	*N*
Nom.	fēlīx	fēlīx	fēlīx	fēlicēs	fēlicēs	fēlicia
Voc.	fēlīx	fēlīx	fēlīx	fēlicēs	fēlicēs	fēlicia
Acc.	fēlicem	fēlicem	fēlīx	fēlicēs	fēlicēs	fēlicia
Gen.	fēlicis	fēlicis	fēlicis	fēlicium	fēlicium	fēlicium
Dat.	fēlicī	fēlicī	fēlicī	fēlicibus	fēlicibus	fēlicibus
Abl.	fēlicī	fēlicī	fēlicī	fēlicibus	fēlicibus	fēlicibus

Declined like ingēns or fēlīx are,

audāx, *bold*	**prūdēns,** *prudent*
ferōx, *fierce*	**trux,** *grim.*
sapiēns, *wise*	

(b) Adjectives with **two** endings in the **Nominative Singular.**

brevis – brevis – breve, *short, brief.*

	SINGULAR			PLURAL		
	M	*F*	*N*	*M*	*F*	*N*
Nom.	brevis	brevis	breve	brevēs	brevēs	brevia
Voc.	brevis	brevis	breve	brevēs	brevēs	brevia
Acc.	brevem	brevem	breve	brevēs	brevēs	brevia
Gen.	brevis	brevis	brevis	brevium	brevium	brevium
Dat.	brevī	brevī	brevī	brevibus	brevibus	brevibus
Abl.	brevī	brevī	brevī	brevibus	brevibus	brevibus

Declined like brevis are,

facilis, *easy*   **omnis,** *all, every*
difficilis, *difficult*   **dulcis,** *sweet*
fortis, *brave*   **trīstis,** *sad*
levis, *light*   **tālis,** *such a kind*
gravis, *heavy*   **quālis,** *what kind of.*

(c) Adjectives with **three** endings in the **Nominative Singular.**

celer – celeris – celere, *swift.*

	SINGULAR			PLURAL		
	M	*F*	*N*	*M*	*F*	*N*
Nom.	celer	celeris	celere	celerēs	celerēs	celeria
Voc.	celer	celeris	celere	celerēs	celerēs	celeria
Acc.	celerem	celerem	celere	celerēs	celerēs	celeria
Gen.	celeris	celeris	celeris	celerium	celerium	celerium
Dat.	celerī	celerī	celerī	celeribus	celeribus	celeribus
Abl.	celerī	celerī	celerī	celeribus	celeribus	celeribus

ācer – ācris – ācre, *keen.*

	SINGULAR			PLURAL		
	M	*F*	*N*	*M*	*F*	*N*
Nom.	ācer	ācris	ācre	ācrēs	ācrēs	acria
Voc.	ācer	ācris	ācre	ācrēs	ācrēs	acria
Acc.	ācrem	ācrem	ācre	ācrēs	ācrēs	acria
Gen.	ācris	ācris	ācris	ācrium	ācrium	ācrium
Dat.	ācrī	ācrī	ācrī	ācribus	ācribus	ācribus
Abl.	ācrī	ācrī	ācrī	ācribus	ācribus	ācribus

(d) Exceptions

vetus – vetus – vetus, *old.*

	SINGULAR			PLURAL		
	M	F	N	M	F	N
Nom.	vetus	vetus	vetus	veterēs	veterēs	vetera
Voc.	vetus	vetus	vetus	veterēs	veterēs	vetera
Acc.	veterem	veterem	vetus	veterēs	veterēs	vetera
Gen.	veteris	veteris	veteris	veterum	veterum	veterum
Dat.	veterī	veterī	veterī	veteribus	veteribus	veteribus
Abl.	vetere	vetere	vetere	veteribus	veteribus	veteribus

Declined like vetus are,

pauper – pauperis, *poor*
dīves – dīvitis, *rich* } no Neuter.

(e) The **Present Participle** declines like **ingēns.** If it is used as an Adjective, its Ablative Singular is **–ī**; if it is used as a pure participle, i.e. in an Ablative Absolute, its Ablative Singular is **–e.**

> e.g. ā puerō errantī – *by the wandering boy*
> vēre ineunte – *at the approach of spring.*

(f) *Declension of the Comparative*
pulchrior – pulchrior – pulchrius, *more beautiful.*

	SINGULAR		
	M	F	N
Nom.	pulchrior	pulchrior	pulchrius
Voc.	pulchrior	pulchrior	pulchrius
Acc.	pulchriōrem	pulchriōrem	pulchrius
Gen.	pulchriōris	pulchriōris	pulchriōris
Dat.	pulchriōrī	pulchriōrī	pulchriōrī
Abl.	pulchriōre	pulchriōre	pulchriōre

	PLURAL		
	M	F	N
Nom.	pulchriōrēs	pulchriōrēs	pulchriōra
Voc.	pulchriōrēs	pulchriōrēs	pulchriōra
Acc.	pulchriōrēs	pulchriōrēs	pulchriōra
Gen.	pulchriōrum	pulchriōrum	pulchriōrum
Dat.	pulchriōribus	pulchriōribus	pulchriōribus
Abl.	pulchriōribus	pulchriōribus	pulchriōribus

(g) The following rule may be observed.

Third Declension Adjectives have their Ablative Singular in –ī

Nominative, Vocative and Accusative Neuter Plural in –ia
Genitive Plural in –ium.

Except, dīves, pauper, vetus and all Comparatives which have their

Ablative Singular in –e

Nominative, Vocative and Accusative Neuter Plural in –a

Genitive Plural in –um.

20. COMPARISON OF ADJECTIVES

To form the **Comparative** of the regular Adjective change the –ī or –is of the Masculine Genitive Singular into –ior and into –issimus to form the **Superlative**.

(a)

POSITIVE	COMPARATIVE	SUPERLATIVE	
altus	alt**ior**	alt**issimus**	*high*
prūdēns	prūdent**ior**	prūdent**issimus**	*prudent*
ferōx	ferōc**ior**	ferōc**issimus**	*fierce*
dulcis	dulc**ior**	dulc**issimus**	*sweet*

(b) If the Adjective ends in –er in the Masculine Nominative Singular, double the –r and add –imus to form the **Superlative**.

POSITIVE	COMPARATIVE	SUPERLATIVE	
miser	miser**ior**	miser**rimus**	*wretched*
pulcher	pulchr**ior**	pulcher**rimus**	*beautiful*
ācer	ācr**ior**	ācer**rimus**	*keen*
celer	celer**ior**	celer**rimus**	*swift*

(c) There are **six** Adjectives ending in –ilis which double the –l and change the –is into –imus to form the **Superlative**.

POSITIVE	COMPARITIVE	SUPERLATIVE	
facilis	facil**ior**	facil**limus**	*easy*
difficilis	difficil**ior**	difficil**limus**	*difficult*
similis	simil**ior**	simil**limus**	*similar*
dissimilis	dissimil**ior**	dissimil**limus**	*dissimilar*
gracilis	gracil**ior**	gracil**limus**	*slender*
humilis	humil**ior**	humil**limus**	*humble*
But nōbilis	nōbil**ior**	nōbil**issimus**	*noble*
ūtilis	ūtil**ior**	ūtil**issimus**	*useful*

(d) Irregular Comparison

POSITIVE	COMPARATIVE	SUPERLATIVE	
bonus	**melior**	**optimus**	*good*
malus	**pēior**	**pessimus**	*bad*
multus	**plūs**	**plūrimus**	*much*
multī	**plūrēs**	**plūrimī**	*many*
magnus	**māior**	**maximus**	*great*
parvus	**minor**	**minimus**	*small*
dubius	**magis dubius**	**maximē dubius**	*doubtful*
idōneus	**magis idōneus**	**maximē idōneus**	*suitable*

N.B. If the Adjective ends in **-us** preceded by a vowel, it compares with **magis** and **maximē**, but **antīquus**, *ancient* is regular.

     antīquus   antīqu**ior**   antīqu**issimus**   *ancient*

21. COMPARISON OF ADVERBS

The **Comparative** of an **Adverb** is the **same** as the **Neuter Nominative Singular** of the **Comparative Adjective.** To form the **Superlative,** change the **-us** of the **Superlative Adjective** into **-ē.**

(a)

POSITIVE	COMPARATIVE	SUPERLATIVE	
ferōciter	ferōc**ius**	ferōcissim**ē**	*fiercely*
facile	facil**ius**	facillim**ē**	*easily*
difficulter	difficil**ius**	difficillim**ē**	*with difficulty*
miserē	miser**ius**	miserrim**ē**	*wretchedly*
ācriter	ācr**ius**	ācerrim**ē**	*keenly*

(b)

POSITIVE	COMPARATIVE	SUPERLATIVE	
bene	mel**ius**	optim**ē**	*well*
male	pē**ius**	pessim**ē**	*badly*
magnopere	**magis**	maxim**ē**	*greatly*
paulum	min**us**	minim**ē**	*little*
saepe	saep**ius**	saepissim**ē**	*often*
diū	diūt**ius**	diūtissim**ē**	*for a long time*
prope	prop**ius**	proxim**ē**	*near*

III. PRONOUNS

22. (a) **ego,** *I.*   **tū,** *you.*

	SINGULAR	PLURAL	SINGULAR	PLURAL
Nom.	eg**o**	nōs	tū	vōs
Acc.	mē	nōs	tē	vōs
Gen.	meī	nostrum, nostrī	tuī	vestrum, vestrī
Dat.	mihi	nōbīs	tibi	vōbīs
Abl.	mē	nōbīs	tē	vōbīs

meus – a – um, *my*   **noster – tra – trum,** *our*

tuus – a – um, *your*   **vester – tra – trum,** *your*

(b) **is – ea – id,** *he, she, it, that.*

	SINGULAR			PLURAL		
	M	F	N	M	F	N
Nom.	is	ea	id	eī	eae	ea
Acc.	eum	eam	id	eōs	eās	ea
Gen.	ēius	ēius	ēius	eōrum	eārum	eōrum
Dat.	eī	eī	eī	eīs	eīs	eīs
Abl.	eō	eā	eō	eīs	eīs	eīs

N.B. **ēius** means *his, her, its;* **eōrum,** etc., means *their;*
suus – a – um means *his own,* etc.

(c) **hīc – haec – hōc,** *this.*

	SINGULAR			PLURAL		
	M	F	N	M	F	N
Nom.	hīc	haec	hōc	hī	hae	haec
Acc.	hunc	hanc	hōc	hōs	hās	haec
Gen.	hūius	hūius	hūius	hōrum	hārum	hōrum
Dat.	huīc	huīc	huīc	hīs	hīs	hīs
Abl.	hōc	hāc	hōc	hīs	hīs	hīs

(d)   **ille – illa – illud,** *that.*

| | SINGULAR | | | PLURAL | | |
	M	F	N	M	F	N
Nom.	ille	illa	illud	illī	illae	illa
Acc.	illum	illam	illud	illōs	illās	illa
Gen.	illīus	illīus	illīus	illōrum	illārum	illōrum
Dat.	illī	illī	illī	illīs	illīs	illīs
Abl.	illō	illā	illō	illīs	illīs	illīs

(e)   **īdem – eadem – idem,** *the same.*

| | SINGULAR | | | PLURAL | | |
	M	F	N	M	F	N
Nom.	īdem	eadem	idem	eīdem	eaedem	eadem
Acc.	eundem	eandem	idem	eōsdem	eāsdem	eadem
Gen.	ēiusdem	ēiusdem	ēiusdem	eōrundem	eārundem	eōrundem
Dat.	eīdem	eīdem	eīdem	eīsdem	eīsdem	eīsdem
Abl.	eōdem	eādem	eōdem	eīsdem	eīsdem	eīsdem

(f) **mē,** *myself.* **tē,** *yourself.* **nōs,** *ourselves.*   **vōs,** *yourselves.*

Acc.	mē	tē	nōs	vōs
Gen.	meī	tuī	nostrī, nostrum	vestrum, vestrī
Dat.	mihi	tibi	nōbīs	vōbīs
Abl.	mē	tē	nōbīs	vōbīs

sē, *himself, herself, themselves.*

Acc.	sē
Gen.	suī
Dat.	sibi
Abl.	sē

(g)   **ipse – ipsa – ipsum,** *self.*

| | SINGULAR | | | PLURAL | | |
	M	F	N	M	F	N
Nom.	ipse	ipsa	ipsum	ipsī	ipsae	ipsa
Acc.	ipsum	ipsam	ipsum	ipsōs	ipsās	ipsa
Gen.	ipsīus	ipsīus	ipsīus	ipsōrum	ipsārum	ipsōrum
Dat.	ipsī	ipsī	ipsī	ipsīs	ipsīs	ipsīs
Abl.	ipsō	ipsā	ipsō	ipsīs	ipsīs	ipsīs

(h)   **quī – quae – quod,** *who, which.*

	SINGULAR			PLURAL		
	M	*F*	*N*	*M*	*F*	*N*
Nom.	quī	quae	quod	quī	quae	quae
Acc.	quem	quam	quod	quōs	quās	quae
Gen.	cūius	cūius	cūius	quōrum	quārum	quōrum
Dat.	cuī	cuī	cuī	quibus	quibus	quibus
Abl.	quō	quā	quō	quibus	quibus	quibus

N.B. quīdam – quaedam – quoddam, *a certain*
  quīcunque – quaecunque – quodcunque, *whoever.*
  The Interrogative Adjective

  quī
  quis } **– quae – quod,** *what, which?*

                          decline like **quī – quae – quod**

(i)   **quis – quis – quid,** *who, what?*

	SINGULAR			PLURAL		
	M	*F*	*N*	*M*	*F*	*N*
Nom.	quis	quis	quid	quī	quae	quae
Acc.	quem	quam	quid	quōs	quās	quae
Gen.	cūius	cūius	cūius	quōrum	quārum	quōrum
Dat.	cuī	cuī	cuī	quibus	quibus	quibus
Abl.	quō	quā	quō	quibus	quibus	quibus

N.B. aliquis – aliqua – aliquid, *someone*
  quisquis – quisquis – quidc } **quid,** *whoever*

  quisquam – quisquam – quicquam, *anyone*
  quisque – quisque – quidc } **que,** *each*

                          are declined like **quis – quis – quid**

(j)   **nēmō,** *no one.*

Nom.	nēmō
Acc.	nēminem
Gen.	nūllīus
Dat.	nēminī
Abl.	nūllō

IV. VERBS

23. Latin Verbs are divided into four groups called **Conjugations.** Every regular Verb has four principal parts from which all other parts may be formed.

First Conjugation: **amō – amāre – amāvī – amātum,** *to love.*

Second Conjugation: **moneō – monēre – monuī – monitum,** *to warn.*

Third Conjugation: **regō – regere – rēxī – rēctum,** *to rule.*

Fourth Conjugation: **audiō – audīre – audīvī – audītum,** *to hear.*

There is also another group of Verbs ending in **–io** which belong to the Third Conjugation:

e.g. **capiō – capere – cēpī – captum,** *to capture.*

Every regular Verb has three stems.

(1) The **Present Stem** is obtained by cutting off the **–re** from the **Present Infinitive Active.**

     e.g. ama~~re~~   monē~~re~~   rege~~re~~   audī~~re~~

(2) The **Perfect Stem** is obtained by cutting off the **–i** from the **Perfect Indicative Active.**

     e.g. amāv~~i~~   monu~~i~~   rēx~~i~~   audīv~~i~~

(3) The **Supine Stem** is obtained by cutting off the **–um** from the **Supine** (Fourth Part).

     e.g. amāt~~um~~   monit~~um~~   rēct~~um~~   audīt~~um~~

The **Present Stem** is used to form the following parts:

Present
Future   } Indicative Active and Passive
Imperfect

Present   } Subjunctive Active and Passive
Imperfect

Present Imperative Active and Passive
Present Infinitive Active and Passive
Present Participle, Gerund and Gerundive.

The **Perfect Stem** is used to form the following parts:
> Perfect and Pluperfect Indicative and Subjunctive Active
> Future Perfect Indicative Active
> Perfect Infinitive Active

The **Supine Stem** is used to form the following parts:
> Perfect and Pluperfect Indicative and Subjunctive Passive
> Future Perfect Indicative Passive
> Perfect Infinitive and Participle Passive
> Future Infinitive Active and Passive and Future Participle

24. (a) *First Conjugation Indicative Active and Passive*
> **amō – amāre – amāvī – amātum,** *to love.*

PRESENT		PERFECT	
ACTIVE	PASSIVE	ACTIVE	PASSIVE
amō	amor	amāvī	amātus sum
amās	amāris	amāvistī	amātus es
amat	amātur	amāvit	amātus est
amāmus	amāmur	amāvimus	amātī sumus
amātis	amāminī	amāvistis	amātī estis
amant	amantur	amāvērunt	amātī sunt

FUTURE		FUTURE PERFECT	
amābō	amābor	amāverō	amātus erō
amābis	amāberis	amāveris	amātus eris
amābit	amābitur	amāverit	amātus erit
amābimus	amābimur	amāverimus	amātī erimus
amābitis	amābiminī	amāveritis	amātī eritis
amābunt	amābuntur	amāverint	amātī erunt

IMPERFECT		PLUPERFECT	
amābam	amābar	amāveram	amātus eram
amābas	amābāris	amāverās	amātus erās
amābat	amābātur	amāverat	amātus erat
amābāmus	amābāmur	amāverāmus	amātī erāmus
amābātis	amābāminī	amāverātis	amātī erātis
amābant	amābantur	amāverant	amātī erant

(b) Second Conjugation Indicative Active and Passive
moneō – monēre – monuī – monitum, *to warn.*

PRESENT		PERFECT	
ACTIVE	PASSIVE	ACTIVE	PASSIVE
moneō	moneor	monuī	monitus sum
monēs	monēris	monuistī	monitus es
monet	monētur	monuit	monitus est
monēmus	monēmur	monuimus	monitī sumus
monētis	monēminī	monuistis	monitī estis
monent	monentur	monuērunt	monitī sunt

FUTURE		FUTURE PERFECT	
monēbō	monēbor	monuerō	monitus erō
monēbis	monēberis	monueris	monitus eris
monēbit	monēbitur	monuerit	monitus erit
monēbimus	monēbimur	monuerimus	monitī erimus
monēbitis	monēbiminī	monueritis	monitī eritis
monēbunt	monēbuntur	monuerint	monitī erunt

IMPERFECT		PLUPERFECT	
monēbam	monēbar	monueram	monitus eram
monēbās	monēbāris	monuerās	monitus erās
monēbat	monēbātur	monuerat	monitus erat
monēbāmus	monēbāmur	monuerāmus	monitī erāmus
monēbātis	monēbāminī	monuerātis	monitī erātis
monēbant	monēbantur	monuerant	monitī erant

(c) Third Conjugation Indicative Active and Passive
regō – regĕre – rēxī – rēctum, *to rule.*

PRESENT		PERFECT	
ACTIVE	PASSIVE	ACTIVE	PASSIVE
regō	regor	rēxī	rēctus sum
regis	regeris	rēxistī	rēctus es
regit	regitur	rēxit	rēctus est
regimus	regimur	rēximus	rēctī sumus
regitis	regiminī	rēxistis	rēctī estis
regunt	reguntur	rēxērunt	rēctī sunt

FUTURE		FUTURE PERFECT	
regam	regar	rēxerō	rēctus erō
regēs	regēris	rēxeris	rēctus eris
reget	regētur	rēxerit	rēctus erit
regēmus	regēmur	rēxerimus	rēctī erimus
regētis	regēminī	rēxeritis	rēctī eritis
regent	regentur	rēxerint	rēctī erunt

IMPERFECT		PLUPERFECT	
regēbam	regēbar	rēxeram	rēctus eram
regēbās	regēbāris	rēxerās	rēctus erās
regēbat	regēbātur	rēxerat	rēctus erat
regēbāmus	regēbāmur	rēxerāmus	rēctī erāmus
regēbātis	regēbāminī	rēxerātis	rēctī erātis
regēbant	regēbantur	rēxerant	rēctī erant

(*d*) *Fourth Conjugation Indicative Active and Passive*
audiō – audīre – audīvī – audītum, *to hear.*

PRESENT			PERFECT	
ACTIVE	PASSIVE	ACTIVE	PASSIVE	
audiō	audior	audīvī	auditus sum	
audīs	audīris	audīvistī	auditus es	
audit	audītur	audīvit	auditus est	
audīmus	audīmur	audīvimus	audītī sumus	
audītis	audīminī	audīvistis	audītī estis	
audiunt	audiuntur	audīvērunt	audītī sunt	

FUTURE		FUTURE PERFECT	
audiam	audiar	audīverō	auditus erō
audiēs	audiēris	audīveris	auditus eris
audiet	audiētur	audīverit	auditus erit
audiēmus	audiēmur	audīverimus	audītī erimus
audiētis	audiēminī	audīveritis	audītī eritis
audient	audientur	audīverint	audītī erunt

IMPERFECT		PLUPERFECT	
audiēbam	audiēbar	audīveram	auditus eram
audiēbās	audiēbāris	audīverās	auditus erās
audiēbat	audiēbātur	audīverat	auditus erat
audiēbāmus	audiēbāmur	audīverāmus	audītī erāmus
audiēbātis	audiēbāminī	audīverātis	audītī erātis
audiēbant	audiēbantur	audīverant	audītī erant

(e) Third Conjugation -io Indicative Active and Passive
capiō – capere – cēpī – captum, *to capture.*

PRESENT		PERFECT	
ACTIVE	PASSIVE	ACTIVE	PASSIVE
capiō	capior	cēpī	captus sum
capis	caperis	cēpistī	captus es
capit	capitur	cēpit	captus est
capimus	capimur	cēpimus	captī sumus
capitis	capiminī	cēpistis	captī estis
capiunt	capiuntur	cēpērunt	captī sunt

FUTURE		FUTURE PERFECT	
capiam	capiar	cēperō	captus erō
capiēs	capiēris	cēperis	captus eris
capiet	capiētur	cēperit	captus erit
capiēmus	capiēmur	cēperimus	captī erimus
capiētis	capiēminī	cēperitis	captī eritis
capient	capientur	cēperint	captī erunt

IMPERFECT		PLUPERFECT	
capiēbam	capiēbar	cēperam	captus eram
capiēbās	capiēbāris	cēperās	captus erās
capiēbat	capiēbātur	cēperat	captus erat
capiēbāmus	capiēbāmur	cēperāmus	captī erāmus
capiēbātis	capiēbāminī	cēperātis	captī erātis
capiēbant	capiēbantur	cēperant	captī erant

25. (a) First Conjugation Subjunctive Active and Passive

PRESENT		PERFECT	
ACTIVE	PASSIVE	ACTIVE	PASSIVE
amem	amer	amāverim	amātus sim
amēs	amēris	amāveris	amātus sīs
amet	amētur	amāverit	amātus sit
amēmus	amēmur	amāverimus	amātī sīmus
amētis	amēminī	amāveritis	amātī sītis
ament	amentur	amāverint	amātī sint

IMPERFECT		PLUPERFECT	
amārem	amārer	amāvissem	amātus essem
amārēs	amārēris	amāvissēs	amātus essēs
amāret	amārētur	amāvisset	amātus esset
amārēmus	amārēmur	amāvissēmus	amātī essēmus
amārētis	amārēminī	amāvissētis	amātī essētis
amārent	amārentur	amāvissent	amātī essent

(b) Second Conjugation Subjunctive Active and Passive

PRESENT		PERFECT	
ACTIVE	PASSIVE	ACTIVE	PASSIVE
moneam	monear	monuerim	monitus sim
moneās	moneāris	monueris	monitus sīs
moneat	moneātur	monuerit	monitus sit
moneāmus	moneāmur	monuerimus	monitī sīmus
moneātis	moneāminī	monueritis	monitī sītis
moneant	moneantur	monuerint	monitī sint

IMPERFECT		PLUPERFECT	
monērem	monērer	monuissem	monitus essem
monērēs	monērēris	monuissēs	monitus essēs
monēret	monērētur	monuisset	monitus esset
monērēmus	monērēmur	monuissēmus	monitī essēmus
monērētis	monērēminī	monuissētis	monitī essētis
monērent	monērentur	monuissent	monitī essent

(c) Third Conjugation Subjunctive Active and Passive

PRESENT		PERFECT	
ACTIVE	PASSIVE	ACTIVE	PASSIVE
regam	regar	rēxerim	rēctus sim
regās	regāris	rēxeris	rēctus sīs
regat	regātur	rēxerit	rēctus sit
regāmus	regāmur	rēxerimus	rēctī sīmus
regātis	regāminī	rēxeritis	rēctī sītis
regant	regantur	rēxerint	rēctī sint

IMPERFECT		PLUPERFECT	
regerem	regerer	rēxissem	rēctus essem
regerēs	regerēris	rēxissēs	rēctus essēs
regeret	regerētur	rēxisset	rēctus esset
regerēmus	regerēmur	rēxissēmus	rēctī essēmus
regerētis	regerēminī	rēxissētis	rēctī essētis
regerent	regerentur	rēxissent	rēctī essent

(d) Fourth Conjugation Subjunctive Active and Passive

PRESENT		PERFECT	
ACTIVE	PASSIVE	ACTIVE	PASSIVE
audiam	audiar	audīverim	audītus sim
audiās	audiāris	audīveris	audītus sīs
audiat	audiātur	audīverit	audītus sit
audiāmus	audiāmur	audīverimus	audītī sīmus
audiātis	audiāminī	audīveritis	audītī sītis
audiant	audiantur	audīverint	audītī sint

IMPERFECT		PLUPERFECT	
audīrem	audīrer	audīvissem	audītus essem
audīrēs	audīrēris	audīvissēs	audītus essēs
audīret	audīrētur	audīvisset	audītus esset
audīrēmus	audīrēmur	audīvissēmus	audītī essēmus
audīrētis	audīrēminī	audīvissētis	audītī essētis
audīrent	audīrentur	audīvissent	audītī essent

(e) Third Conjugation -io Subjunctive Active and Passive

PRESENT		PERFECT	
ACTIVE	PASSIVE	ACTIVE	PASSIVE
capiam	capiar	cēperim	captus sim
capiās	capiāris	cēperis	captus sīs
capiat	capiātur	cēperit	captus sit
capiāmus	capiāmur	cēperimus	captī sīmus
capiātis	capiāminī	cēperitis	captī sītis
capiant	capiantur	cēperint	captī sint

IMPERFECT		PLUPERFECT	
caperem	caperer	cēpissem	captus essem
caperēs	caperēris	cēpissēs	captus essēs
caperet	caperētur	cēpisset	captus esset
caperēmus	caperēmur	cēpissēmus	captī essēmus
caperētis	caperēminī	cēpissētis	captī essētis
caperent	caperentur	cēpissent	captī essent

26. *Imperative Active and Passive All Conjugations*

ACTIVE

FIRST	SECOND	THIRD	FOURTH	-IO
amā	monē	rege	audī	cape
amāte	monēte	regite	audīte	capite

PASSIVE

amāre	monēre	regere	audīre	capere
amāminī	monēminī	regiminī	audīminī	capiminī

27. *Infinitive Active and Passive All Conjugations*

ACTIVE

	FIRST	SECOND	THIRD	FOURTH
Present	amāre	monēre	regere	audīre
Future	amātūrus esse	monitūrus esse	rēctūrus esse	audītūrus esse
Perfect	amāvisse	monuisse	rēxisse	audīvisse

-IO

Present	capere
Future	captūrus esse
Perfect	cēpisse

PASSIVE

	FIRST	SECOND	THIRD	FOURTH	-IO
Present	amārī	monērī	regī	audīrī	capī
Future	amātum īrī	monitum īrī	rēctum īrī	audītum īrī	captum īrī
Perfect	amātus esse	monitus esse	rēctus esse	audītus esse	captus esse

28. *Participles Active and Passive All Conjugations*

ACTIVE

	FIRST	SECOND	THIRD
Present	am**āns–āns–āns**	mon**ēns–ēns–ēns**	reg**ēns–ēns–ēns**
Future	amāt**ūrus–a–um**	monit**ūrus–a–um**	rēct**ūrus–a–um**

	FOURTH	-IO
Present	aud**iēns–iēns–iēns**	cap**iēns–iēns–iēns**
Future	audīt**ūrus–a–um**	capt**ūrus–a–um**

PASSIVE

	FIRST	SECOND	THIRD	FOURTH
Perfect	amāt**us–a–um**	monit**us–a–um**	rēct**us–a–um**	audīt**us–a–um**

	-IO
Perfect	capt**us–a–um**

29. *Gerund and Gerundive All Conjugations*

	FIRST	SECOND	THIRD
Gerund	am**andum**	mon**endum**	reg**endum**
Gerundive	am**andus–a–um**	mon**endus–a–um**	reg**endus–a–um**

	FOURTH	-IO
Gerund	aud**iendum**	cap**iendum**
Gerundive	aud**iendus–a–um**	cap**iendus–a–um**

30. Latin also has the following irregular Verbs which do not conform to any conjugation.

> **sum – esse – fuī,** *to be*
> **possum – posse – potuī,** *to be able*
> **volō – velle – voluī,** *to wish, to be willing*
> **nōlō – nōlle – nōluī,** *to be unwilling*
> **mālō – mālle – māluī,** *to prefer*
> **eō – īre – īvī – itum,** *to go*

ferō – ferre – tulī – lātum, *to bear, carry*
fīō – fierī – factus sum, *to be made, to become.*

31.   **sum – esse – fuī,** *to be.*

INDICATIVE		SUBJUNCTIVE	
PRESENT	PERFECT	PRESENT	PERFECT
sum	fuī	sim	fuerim
es	fuistī	sīs	fueris
est	fuit	sit	fuerit
sumus	fuimus	sīmus	fuerimus
estis	fuistis	sītis	fueritis
sunt	fuērunt	sint	fuerint

FUTURE	FUTURE PERFECT
erō	fuerō
eris	fueris
erit	fuerit
erimus	fuerimus
eritis	fueritis
erunt	fuerint

IMPERFECT	PLUPERFECT	IMPERFECT	PLUPERFECT
eram	fueram	essem	fuissem
erās	fuerās	essēs	fuissēs
erat	fuerat	esset	fuisset
erāmus	fuerāmus	essēmus	fuissēmus
erātis	fuerātis	essētis	fuissētis
erant	fuerant	essent	fuissent

IMPERATIVE	INFINITIVES	PARTICIPLE
es	Present **esse**	Future futūrus–a–um
este	Future futūrus esse (fore)	
	Perfect fuisse	

N.B. The following compound Verbs conjugate like sum.

absum – **abesse** – **āfuī,** *to be distant*
adsum – **adesse** – **adfuī,** *to be present*
dēsum – **dēesse** – **dēfuī,** *to fail, be lacking to* +Dative
īnsum – **inesse** – **īnfui,** *to be in*
intersum – **interesse** – **interfuī,** *to take part in* +Dative
praesum – **praeesse** – **praefuī,** *to be in command of* +Dative
obsum – **obesse** – **obfuī,** *to be of disadvantage to* +Dative
supersum – **superesse** – **superfuī,** *to survive* +Dative

But prōsum – **prōdesse** – **prōfuī,** *to be of advantage to*+
Dative puts in a **–d** where any part of **sum** begins with an **–e.**

e.g. prōsum   Future: prōderō
prōdes   etc.
prōdest

32.   **possum** – **posse** – **potuī,** *to be able, can.*

N.B. This verb is really a compound of **pot**+sum. Where any part of **sum** begins with an **–s,** pot becomes po**s.**

INDICATIVE		SUBJUNCTIVE	
PRESENT	PERFECT	PRESENT	PERFECT
possum	potuī	possim	potuerim
potes	potuistī	possīs	potueris
potest	potuit	possit	potuerit
possumus	potuimus	possīmus	potuerimus
potestis	potuistis	possītis	potueritis
possunt	potuērunt	possint	potuerint

	FUTURE	FUTURE PERFECT
	poterō	potuerō
	poteris	potueris
	poterit	potuerit
	poterimus	potuerimus
	poteritis	potueritis
	poterunt	potuerint

IMPERFECT	PLUPERFECT	IMPERFECT	PLUPERFECT
poteram	potueram	possem	potuissem
poterās	potuerās	possēs	potuissēs
poterat	potuerat	posset	potuisset
poterāmus	potuerāmus	possēmus	potuissēmus
poterātis	potuerātis	possētis	potuissētis
poterant	potuerant	possent	potuissent

INFINITIVES

Present	posse
Perfect	potuisse

33.   volō – velle – voluī, *to be willing, to wish.*

INDICATIVE		SUBJUNCTIVE	
PRESENT	PERFECT	PRESENT	PERFECT
volō	voluī	velim	voluerim
vīs	voluistī	velīs	volueris
vult	voluit	velit	voluerit
volumus	voluimus	velīmus	voluerimus
vultis	voluistis	velītis	volueritis
volunt	voluērunt	velint	voluerint

FUTURE	FUTURE PERFECT
volam	voluerō
volēs	volueris
volet	voluerit
volēmus	voluerimus
volētis	volueritis
volent	voluerint

IMPERFECT	PLUPERFECT	IMPERFECT	PLUPERFECT
volēbam	volueram	vellem	voluissem
volēbās	voluerās	vellēs	voluissēs
volēbat	voluerat	vellet	voluisset
volēbāmus	voluerāmus	vellēmus	voluissēmus
volēbātis	voluerātis	vellētis	voluissētis
volēbant	voluerant	vellent	voluissent

INFINITIVES			PARTICIPLE
Present	velle	Present	volens–ēns–ēns
Perfect	voluisse		

B

34.   **nōlō – nōlle – nōluī,** *to be unwilling.*

INDICATIVE		SUBJUNCTIVE	
PRESENT	PERFECT	PRESENT	PERFECT
nōlō	nōluī	nōlim	nōluerim
nōn vīs	nōluistī	nōlīs	nōlueris
nōn vult	nōluit	nōlit	nōluerit
nōlumus	nōluimus	nōlīmus	nōluerimus
nōn vultis	nōluistis	nōlītis	nōlueritis
nōlunt	nōluērunt	nōlint	nōluerint

	FUTURE	FUTURE PERFECT
	nōlam	nōluerō
	nōlēs	nōlueris
	nōlet	nōluerit
	nōlēmus	nōluerimus
	nōlētis	nōlueritis
	nōlent	nōluerint

IMPERFECT	PLUPERFECT	IMPERFECT	PLUPERFECT
nōlēbam	nōlueram	nōllem	nōluissem
nōlēbās	nōluerās	nōllēs	nōluissēs
nōlēbat	nōluerat	nōllet	nōluisset
nōlēbāmus	nōluerāmus	nōllēmus	nōluissēmus
nōlēbātis	nōluerātis	nōllētis	nōluissētis
nōlēbant	nōluerant	nōllent	nōluissent

IMPERATIVE	INFINITIVES		PARTICIPLE
nōlī	Present	**nōlle**	Present nōlēns–ēns–ēns
nōlīte	Perfect	nōluisse	

35.   **mālo – mālle – māluī,** *to prefer.*

INDICATIVE		SUBJUNCTIVE	
PRESENT	PERFECT	PRESENT	PERFECT
mālō	māluī	mālim	māluerim
māvīs	māluistī	mālīs	mālueris
māvult	māluit	mālit	māluerit
mālumus	māluimus	mālīmus	māluerimus
māvultis	māluistis	mālītis	mālueritis
mālunt	māluērunt	mālint	māluerint

FUTURE	FUTURE PERFECT
mālam	māluerō
mālēs	mālueris
mālet	māluerit
mālēmus	māluerimus
mālētis	mālueritis
mālent	māluerint

IMPERFECT	PLUPERFECT	IMPERFECT	PLUPERFECT
mālēbam	mālueram	māllem	māluissem
mālēbās	māluerās	māllēs	māluissēs
mālēbat	māluerat	māllet	māluisset
mālēbāmus	māluerāmus	māllēmus	māluissēmus
mālēbātis	māluerātis	māllētis	māluissētis
mālēbant	māluerant	māllent	māluissent

INFINITIVES

Present	mālle
Perfect	māluisse

36.   eō – īre – īvī – itum, *to go.*

	INDICATIVE		SUBJUNCTIVE

PRESENT	PERFECT	PRESENT	PERFECT
eō	īvī	eam	īverim
īs	īvistī	eās	īveris
it	īvit	eat	īverit
īmus	īvimus	eāmus	īverimus
ītis	īvistis	eātis	īveritis
eunt	īvērunt	eant	īverint

FUTURE	FUTURE PERFECT
ībō	īverō
ībis	īveris
ībit	īverit
ībimus	īverimus
ībitis	īveritis
ībunt	īverint

IMPERFECT	PLUPERFECT	IMPERFECT	PLUPERFECT
ībam	īveram	īrem	īvissem
ībās	īverās	īrēs	īvissēs
ībat	īverat	īret	īvisset
ībāmus	īverāmus	īrēmus	īvissēmus
ībātis	īverātis	īrētis	īvissētis
ībant	īverant	īrent	īvissent

IMPERATIVE		INFINITIVES		PARTICIPLES
ī	Present	īre	Present	iēns-iēns-iēns (euntis)
īte	Future	itūrus esse	Future	itūrus-a-um
	Perfect	īvisse		
	Gerund	eundum		
	Gerundive	eundum (impersonal)		

N.B. The following compound Verbs are conjugated like **eō**, but drop the **v** in their third part.

> **abeō – abīre – abiī – abitum,** *to go away*
> **adeō – adīre – adiī – aditum,** *to approach*
> **exeō – exīre – exiī – exitum,** *to go out*
> **ineō – inīre – iniī – initum,** *to enter*
> **intereō – interīre – interiī – interitum,** *to perish*
> **obeō – obīre – obiī – obitum,** *meet, die*
> **pereō – perīre – periī – peritum,** *to perish*
> **redeō – redīre – rediī – reditum,** *to return*
> **trānseō – trānsīre – trānsiī – trānsitum,** *to cross.*

37.   **ferō – ferre – tulī – lātum,** *to bear, carry.*

INDICATIVE

PRESENT		PERFECT	
ACTIVE	PASSIVE	ACTIVE	PASSIVE
ferō	feror	tulī	lātus sum
fers	ferris	tulistī	lātus es
fert	fertur	tulit	lātus est
ferimus	ferimur	tulimus	lātī sumus
fertis	feriminī	tulistis	lātī estis
ferunt	feruntur	tulērunt	lātī sunt

FUTURE		FUTURE PERFECT	
feram	ferar	tulerō	lātus erō
ferēs	ferēris	tuleris	lātus eris
feret	ferētur	tulerit	lātus erit
ferēmus	ferēmur	tulerimus	lātī erimus
ferētis	ferēminī	tuleritis	lātī eritis
ferent	ferentur	tulerint	lātī erunt

IMPERFECT		PLUPERFECT	
ACTIVE	PASSIVE	ACTIVE	PASSIVE
ferēbam	ferēbar	tuleram	lātus eram
ferēbās	ferēbāris	tulerās	lātus erās
ferēbat	ferēbātur	tulerat	lātus erat
ferēbāmus	ferēbāmur	tulerāmus	lātī erāmus
ferēbātis	ferēbāminī	tulerātis	lātī erātis
ferēbant	ferēbantur	tulerant	lātī erant

SUBJUNCTIVE

PRESENT		PERFECT	
feram	ferar	tulerim	lātus sim
ferās	ferāris	tuleris	lātus sīs
ferat	ferātur	tulerit	lātus sit
ferāmus	ferāmur	tulerimus	lātī sīmus
ferātis	ferāminī	tuleritis	lātī sītis
ferant	ferantur	tulerint	lātī sint

IMPERFECT		PLUPERFECT	
ferrem	ferrer	tulissem	lātus essem
ferrēs	ferrēris	tulissēs	lātus essēs
ferret	ferrētur	tulisset	lātus esset
ferrēmus	ferrēmur	tulissēmus	lātī essēmus
ferrētis	ferrēminī	tulissētis	lātī essētis
ferrent	ferrentur	tulissent	lātī essent

IMPERATIVE		INFINITIVES		
ACTIVE	PASSIVE		ACTIVE	PASSIVE
fer	ferre	Present	ferre	ferrī
ferte	feriminī	Future	lātūrus esse	lātum īrī
		Perfect	tulisse	lātus esse

PARTICIPLES

Present	ferēns-ēns-ēns	Gerund	ferendum
Future	lātūrus-a-um	Gerundive	ferendus-a-um
Perfect	lātus-a-um		

N.B. The following compound Verbs conjugate like fero.

afferō – afferre – attulī – allātum, *to bring to*
auferō – auferre – abstulī – ablātum, *to take away*
cōnferō – cōnferre – contulī – collātum, *to bring together*
efferō – efferre – extulī – ēlātum, *to bring out*
referō – referre – rettulī – relātum, *to bring back*

38. fīō – fierī – factus sum, *to be made, to become.*

INDICATIVE		SUBJUNCTIVE	
PRESENT	PERFECT	PRESENT	PERFECT
fīō	factus sum	fīam	factus sim
fīs	factus es	fīās	factus sīs
fit	factus est	fīat	factus sit
—	factī sumus	fīāmus	factī sīmus
—	factī estis	fīātis	factī sītis
fīunt	factī sunt	fīant	factī sint
	FUTURE		FUTURE PERFECT
	fīam		factus erō
	fīēs		factus eris
	fīet		factus erit
	fīēmus		factī erimus
	fīētis		factī eritis
	fīent		factī erunt
IMPERFECT	PLUPERFECT	IMPERFECT	PLUPERFECT
fīēbam	factus eram	fierem	factus essem
fīēbās	factus erās	fierēs	factus essēs
fīēbat	factus erat	fieret	factus esset
fīēbāmus	factī erāmus	fierēmus	factī essēmus
fīēbātis	factī erātis	fierētis	factī essētis
fīēbant	factī erant	fierent	factī essent

INFINITIVES		PARTICIPLE	
Present	fierī		
Future	factum īrī	Perfect	factus-a-um
Perfect	factus esse	Gerundive	faciendus-a-um

39. *Deponent Verbs*

These Verbs are **Active** in meaning, but **Passive** in form except for the **Present Participle** ⎫ which are **Active** in
Future Infinitive ⎬ form.
Future Participle ⎭

N.B. The **Perfect Participle** of a **Deponent Verb** is **Active** in meaning.

(*a*) *First Conjugation*

hortor – hortārī – hortātus sum, *to encourage.*

INDICATIVE		SUBJUNCTIVE	
PRESENT	PERFECT	PRESENT	PERFECT
hortor	hortātus sum	horter	hortātus sim
hortāris	hortātus es	hortēris	hortātus sīs
etc.	etc.	etc.	etc.

	FUTURE	FUTURE PERFECT
	hortābor	hortātus erō
	hortāberis	hortātus eris
	etc.	etc.

IMPERFECT	PLUPERFECT	IMPERFECT	PLUPERFECT
hortābar	hortātus eram	hortārer	hortātus essem
hortābāris	hortātus erās	hortārēris	hortātus essēs
etc.	etc.	etc.	etc.

IMPERATIVE	INFINITIVES	
hortāre	Present	hortārī
hortāminī	Future	hortātūrus esse
	Perfect	hortātus esse

PARTICIPLES

Present	hortāns-āns-āns	Gerund	hortandum
Future	hortātūrus-a-um	Gerundive	hortandus–a–um
Perfect	hortātus-a-um		
	(**Active** in meaning)		

(b) Second Conjugation

vereor – verērī – veritus sum, *to fear.*

INDICATIVE		SUBJUNCTIVE	
PRESENT	PERFECT	PRESENT	PERFECT
vereor	veritus sum	verear	veritus sim
verēris	veritus es	vereāris	veritus sīs
etc.	etc.	etc.	etc.
	FUTURE	FUTURE PERFECT	
	verēbor	veritus erō	
	verēberis	veritus eris	
	etc.	etc.	
IMPERFECT	PLUPERFECT	IMPERFECT	PLUPERFECT
verēbar	veritus eram	verērer	veritus essem
verēbāris	veritus erās	verērēris	veritus essēs
etc.	etc.	etc.	etc.

IMPERATIVE		INFINITIVES	
verēre	Present	verērī	
verēminī	Future	veritūrus esse	
	Perfect	veritus esse	

PARTICIPLES

Present	verēns-ēns-ēns	Gerund	verendum
Future	veritūrus-a-um	Gerundive	verendus-a-um
Perfect	veritus-a-um		

(**Active** in meaning)

(c) Third Conjugation

proficīscor – proficīscī – profectus sum, *to set out.*

INDICATIVE		SUBJUNCTIVE	
PRESENT	PERFECT	PRESENT	PERFECT
proficīscor	profectus sum	proficīscar	profectus sim
proficīsceris	profectus es	proficīscāris	profectus sīs
etc.	etc.	etc.	etc.
	FUTURE	FUTURE PERFECT	
	proficīscar	profectus erō	
	proficīscēris	profectus eris	
	etc.	etc.	

IMPERFECT	PLUPERFECT	IMPERFECT	PLUPERFECT
proficīscēbar	profectus eram	proficīscerer	profectus essem
proficīscēbāris	profectus erās	proficīscerēris	profectus essēs
etc.	etc.	etc.	etc.

	IMPERATIVE		INFINITIVES	
	proficīscere	Present	proficīscī	
	proficīsciminī	Future	profectūrus esse	
		Perfect	profectus esse	

PARTICIPLES

Present	proficīscēns-ēns-ēns	Gerund	proficīscendum
Future	profectūrus-a-um	Gerundive	proficīscendum
Perfect	profectus-a-um		(Impersonal)
	(**Active** in meaning)		

(*d*) *Fourth Conjugation*

mentior – mentīrī – mentītus sum, *to tell a lie.*

INDICATIVE		SUBJUNCTIVE	
PRESENT	PERFECT	PRESENT	PERFECT
mentior	mentītus sum	mentiar	mentītus sim
mentīris	mentītus es	mentiāris	mentītus sīs
etc.	etc.	etc.	etc.

	FUTURE	FUTURE PERFECT
	mentiar	mentītus erō
	mentiēris	mentītus eris
	etc.	etc.

IMPERFECT	PLUPERFECT	IMPERFECT	PLUPERFECT
mentiēbar	mentītus eram	mentīrer	mentītus essem
mentiēbāris	mentītus erās	mentīrēris	mentītus essēs
etc.	etc.	etc.	etc.

	IMPERATIVE		INFINITIVES
	mentīre	Present	mentīrī
	mentīminī	Future	mentītūrus esse
		Perfect	mentītus esse

PARTICIPLES

Present	mentiēns-iēns-iēns	Gerund	mentiendum
Future	mentītūrus-a-um	Gerundive	mentiendum
Perfect	mentītus-a-um		(Impersonal)
	(**Active** in meaning)		

(e) *Third Conjugation* – **ior**
morior – morī – mortuus sum, *to die.*

INDICATIVE		SUBJUNCTIVE	
PRESENT	PERFECT	PRESENT	PERFECT
mor**ior**	mor**tuus sum**	mor**iar**	mor**tuus sim**
mor**eris**	mor**tuus es**	mor**iāris**	mor**tuus sīs**
etc.	etc.	etc.	etc.
	FUTURE	FUTURE PERFECT	
	mor**iar**	mor**tuus erō**	
	mor**iēris**	mor**tuus eris**	
	etc.	etc.	
IMPERFECT	PLUPERFECT	IMPERFECT	PLUPERFECT
mor**iēbar**	mor**tuus eram**	mor**erer**	mor**tuus essem**
mor**iēbāris**	mor**tuus eras**	mor**erēris**	mor**tuus essēs**
etc.	etc.	etc.	etc.

IMPERATIVE		INFINITIVES	
mor**ere**	Present	mor**ī**	
mor**iminī**	Future	mor**itūrus esse**	
	Perfect	mor**tuus esse**	

PARTICIPLES

Present	mor**iēns-iēns-iēns**	Gerund	mor**iendum**
Future	mor**itūrus-a-um**	Gerundive	mor**iendum**
Perfect	mor**tuus-a-um**		(Impersonal)
	(Active in meaning)		

40. *Semi-Deponent Verbs*

Latin has four Verbs **Active** in meaning which are **Active** in form in the **Present, Future and Imperfect tenses,** but **Passive** in form in the **Perfect Tenses.**

> **audeō – audēre – ausus sum,** *to dare*
> **gaudeō – gaudēre – gāvīsus sum,** *to rejoice*
> **soleō – solēre – solitus sum,** *to be accustomed to*
> **(cōn)fīdō – fīdĕre – fīsus sum,** *to trust.*

e.g.   INDICATIVE   SUBJUNCTIVE

PRESENT	PERFECT	PRESENT	PERFECT
audeō	ausus **sum**	aud**eam**	ausus **sim**
audēs	ausus **ēs**	aud**eās**	ausus **sīs**
etc.	etc.	etc.	etc.

	FUTURE	FUTURE PERFECT	
	audē**bō**	ausus **erō**	
	audē**bis**	ausus **eris**	
	etc.	etc.	

IMPERFECT	PLUPERFECT	IMPERFECT	PLUPERFECT
audē**bam**	ausus **eram**	audē**rem**	ausus **essem**
audē**bās**	ausus **erās**	audē**rēs**	ausus **essēs**
etc.	etc.	etc.	etc.

IMPERATIVE   INFINITIVES

	audē	Present	audēre
	audēte	Future	ausūrus esse
		Perfect	ausus esse

PARTICIPLES

Present	audēns-ēns-ēns	Gerund	aud**endum**
Future	ausūrus-a-um	Gerundive	aud**endus-a-um**
Perfect	ausus-a-um		

(**Active** in meaning)

V. PREPOSITIONS

41. *With Accusative*

ad: to, towards, at, with regard to, about (of numbers)

ad castra redīre: *to return to the camp.*
ad iānuam manēre: *to stay at the door.*
ad virtūtem: *with regard to courage.*
ad tempus: *in time.*
ad centum: *about an hundred.*

ante: before

ante portam: *before the gate.*
ante prīmam lūcem: *before dawn.*

apud: at the house of, in the writings of, before (of persons)
    apud mē: *at my house.*
    apud Cicerōnem: *in the writings of.*
    apud iūdicem: *before the judge.*

contrā: against, opposite to
    contrā hostēs: *against the enemy.*

    īnsula contrā Britanniam sita: *an island* $\begin{cases} opposite\ Britain. \\ lying\ off\ Britain. \end{cases}$

extrā: outside of
    extrā tēlī iactum: *out of range.*
    extrā ordinem: *out of turn.*
    extrā urbem: *outside the city.*

in: into, against
    in Italiam: *into Italy.*

    in hostēs impetum facere: *to make an attack* $\begin{cases} against \\ on \\ upon \end{cases}$ *the enemy.*

inter: between, among, during
    inter rīpās: *between the banks.*
    inter sē pugnābant: *they fought with each other.*
    inter proelium: *during the battle.*

intrā: within
    intrā moenia: *within the walls.*
    intrā tēlī iactum: *within range.*

ob: on account of
    quam ob rem: *therefore.*
    ob hanc causam: *for this reason.*

per: through, during, by means of, by (in oaths)
    per mediam urbem: *through the middle of the city.*
    per noctem: *during the night.*
    per servum: *by means of a slave.*
    per ego tē deōs ōrō: *I beg you by the gods.*

post: behind, after
    post tergum: *in the rear.*
    post hominum memoriam: *within human memory.*

praeter: past, beyond, except, contrary to
    praeter urbem: *past the city.*

praeter spem: *beyond expectation.*
praeter ducem: *except the general.*
praeter cōnsuētūdinem: *contrary to custom.*

prope: near
prope casam: *near the cottage.*

propter: on account of
propter vulnera: *on account of the wounds.*

secundum: in accordance with
$$\left.\begin{array}{l}\text{secundum flūmen} \\ \text{secundō flūmine}\end{array}\right\}:\textit{ downstream.}$$

sub: under (of motion), immediately after
sub iugum mittere: *to send under the yoke.*
sub bellum: *immediately after the war.*

trāns: across
trāns flūmen: *across the river.*

ultrā: beyond
ultrā collem: *beyond the hill.*

42. *With Ablative*

a(b): by, from, in relation to
ā mīlite: *by the soldier.*
ā Rōmā decem mīlia passuum abest: *he is ten miles distant from Rome.*
ā puerō: *from boyhood.*
ā tergō, fronte, latere: *in the rear, front, flank.*
ā Caesare stāre: *to be on the side of Caesar.*

cum: with, along with
mēcum festīnā: *hurry with me.*
cum librīs ad ludum veniet: *he will come to school with his books.*
summā cum vī: *with the utmost force.*

dē: down from, about, according to
dē ponte: *down from the bridge.*
dē pāce agere: *to discuss peace.*
dē industriā: *on purpose.*
dē mōre: *according to custom.*
dē imprōvīsō: *unexpectedly.*
dē integrō: *afresh.*

ē(x): from, out of, according to

ē Britanniā nāvigāre: *to sail from Britain.*
ē castrīs exīre: *to go out of the camp.*
ē senātūs cōnsultō: *according to the decree of the senate.*
sex ē mīlitibus: *six of the soldiers.*
statua ex aurō facta: *a statue made of gold.*

in: in, on, in the case of

in urbe manēre: *to stay in the city.*
in capite vulnerārī: *to be wounded on the head.*
in Cicerōne: *in the case of Cicero.*

pro: on behalf of, in front of, in proportion to, as

prō patriā: *on behalf of one's country.*
prō castrīs: *in front of the camp.*
prō virīlī parte pugnāre: *to fight to the best of one's ability.*
prō inimīcō tē habeō: *I regard you as an enemy.*

sine: without

sine scūtō: *without a shield.*

sub: under

sub marī: *under the sea.*
sub hastā vendere: *to sell at an auction.*
sub corōnā vendere: *to sell as a slave.*

VI. NUMBERS

43.

		CARDINAL	ORDINAL
1	I	ūn**us-a-um**	prīm**us-a-um**
2	II	du**o-ae-o**	secund**us-a-um** (alter)
3	III	trēs-ēs-ia	terti**us-a-um**
4	IV	quattuor	quart**us-a-um**
5	V	quīnque	quīnt**us-a-um**
6	VI	sex	sext**us-a-um**
7	VII	septem	septim**us-a-um**
8	VIII	octō	octāv**us-a-um**
9	IX	novem	nōn**us-a-um**
10	X	decem	decim**us-a-um**
11	XI	ūndecim	ūndecim**us-a-um**

		CARDINAL	ORDINAL
12	XII	duodecim	duodecimus-a-um
13	XIII	tredecim	tertius decimus-a-um
14	XIV	quattuordecim	quartus decimus-a-um
15	XV	quīndecim	quīntus decimus-a-um
16	XVI	sēdecim	sextus decimus-a-um
17	XVII	septendecim	septimus decimus-a-um
18	XVIII	duodēvīgintī	duodēvīcēsimus-a-um
19	XIX	ūndēvīgintī	ūndēvīcēsimus-a-um
20	XX	vīgintī	vīcēsimus-a-um
21	XXI	vīgintī ūnus	vīcēsimus prīmus
		(ūnus et vīgintī)	(ūnus et vīcēsimus)
22	XXII	vīgintī duo	vīcēsimus secundus
		(duo et vīgintī)	(alter et vīcēsimus)
30	XXX	trīgintā	trīcēsimus
40	XL	quadrāgintā	quadrāgēsimus
50	L	quīnquāgintā	quīnquāgēsimus
60	LX	sexāgintā	sexāgēsimus
70	LXX	septuāgintā	septuāgēsimus
80	LXXX	octōgintā	octōgēsimus
90	XC	nōnāgintā	nōnāgēsimus
100	C	centum	centēsimus
200	CC	ducentī-ae-a	ducentēsimus
300	CCC	trecentī-ae-a	trecentēsimus
400	CCCC	quadringentī-ae-a	quadringentēsimus
500	D(IↃ)	quīngentī-ae-a	quīngentēsimus
600	DC	sescentī-ae-a	sescentēsimus
700	DCC	septingentī-ae-a	septingentēsimus
800	DCCC	octingentī-ae-a	octingentēsimus
900	DCCCC	nōngentī-ae-a	nōngentēsimus
1000	M(CIↃ)	mīlle	mīllēsimus
2000	MM	duo mīlia	bis mīllēsimus

N.B. (i) The numbers, **1, 2, 3** are declinable, **4 to 100** are indeclinable. For the declension of **ūnus** vid. sec. 18.

duo – duae – duo   tres – tres – tria

	M	*F*	*N*	*M*	*F*	*N*
Nom.	duo	duae	duo	tres	tres	tria
Acc.	duōs (duo)	duās	duo	tres	tres	tria
Gen.	duōrum	duārum	duōrum	trium	trium	trium
Dat.	duōbus	duābus	duōbus	tribus	tribus	tribus
Abl.	duōbus	duābus	duōbus	tribus	tribus	tribus

ambo – ambae – ambo, *both* declines like **duo**

    (ii) **Mīlle,** *a thousand* is indeclinable, but **mīlia,** *thousands* declines thus:

Nom.	mīlia
Acc.	mīlia
Gen.	mīlium
Dat.	mīlibus
Abl.	mīlibus

Mīlia is always followed by the Genitive.

e.g. cum mīlle nōngentīs nōnāgintā novem mīlitibus;
with 1,999 soldiers.

but, cum duōbus mīlibus **mīlitum**;
with 2,000 soldiers.

VII. DATES

44. (*a*) *Names of the Months*

Iānuārius-a-um	(Ian.)	Iūlius-a-um	(Iul.)
Februārius-a-um	(Feb.)	Augustus-a-um	(Aug.)
Martius-a-um	(Mart.)	September-bris-bre	(Sept.)
Aprīlis-is-e	(Apr.)	Octōber-bris-bre	(Oct.)
Māius-a-um	(Mai.)	November-bris-bre	(Nov.)
Iūnius-a-um	(Iun.)	December-bris-bre	(Dec.)

July and August were also known as Quīntīlis-is-e and Sextīlis-is-e.

(b) *Divisions of the Months*

Kalend**ae-ārum** (f. pl.) 1st of every month.

Nōn**ae-ārum** (f. pl.) 5th of the month, except in March, July, October, May when the Nones fell on the 7th day.

Īd**ūs-uum** (f. pl.) 13th of the month, except in March, July, October, May when the Ides fell on the 15th day.

(c) *How to express a date in Latin*

(i) If the date to be expressed falls on one of the divisions use a plain **Ablative** of **Time.**

e.g. *1st Dec.* Kal. Dec. (Kalendīs Decembribus)
15th March. Id. Mart. (Īdibus Martiīs)

(ii) If the date to be expressed falls on the day before one of the divisions use **prīd. (prīdiē)** thus:

4th Feb. **prīd.** Nōn. Feb. (**prīdiē** Nōnās Februāriās)

(iii) If the date to be expressed falls between one of the divisions, subtract the English date from the date of the **next** Latin division, and since the Romans counted inclusively **add one** (**add** on **two** when calculating to the **Kalends** of the **next** month).

e.g. *9th Dec.* **a.d.V.** Īd. Dec.
(ante diem quīntum Īdūs Decembrēs)
16th April. **a.d.XVI** Kal. Māi.
(ante diem sextum decimum Kalendās Māiās)

N.B. Never write a.d.II. This means you have missed a division.

Additional Accidence

VIII. NOUNS

45. *Second Declension*

(*a*) Nouns ending in **-ius** or **-ium** have their **Genitive Singular** in **-ī** or **-iī.**

e.g. **fīlius,** has fīlī or fīliī
praemium, has praemī or praemiī

(*b*) Many cities and countries ending in **-us** are **Feminine.**

e.g. Corinth**us,** *Corinth*
Aegypt**us,** *Egypt*

Humus, *the ground* is also **Feminine,** but **pelagus,** *sea* and **vulgus,** *mob* are **Neuter.**

(*c*) **Sēstertius,** *sesterce* (a coin) has a contracted **Genitive Plural,** sēstertium. This form of the Genitive Plural is very common in poetry, e.g. de**um** for deōrum, vir**um** for virōrum. It is also found in the Genitive Plural of the hundreds, e.g. ducent**um.**

(*d*) **Locus-ī** (m), *place* has two Plurals, loca-ōrum (n), *places, localities,* and locī-ōrum (m), *topics, passages in a book.*

46. *Third Declension*

(*a*) Names of towns and rivers ending in **-is** have their **Accusative Singular** in **-im** and their **Ablative Singular** in **-ī.**

e.g. **Neăpolis,** *Naples* has Neăpolim and Neăpolī
    Tiberis, *Tiber* has Tiberim and Tiberī
Also **puppis-is** (f), *stern of a ship*
    turris-is (f), *tower*
    secūris-is (f), *axe*

Other nouns such as **nāvis-is** (f), *ship* and **ignis-is** (m), *fire* have both forms of the **Ablative Singular, -e** or **-ī**.

(*b*) Nouns such as **pēs-pedis** (m), *foot,* **pāx-pācis** (f), *peace,* **ōs-ōris** (n), *mouth* do **not** belong to the Monosyllabic Group as their stems do not end in two consonants and therefore have **-um** in the **Genitive Plural.**

(*c*) **Mānēs** (m pl), *spirits of the dead,* and **Penātēs** (m pl) *household gods,* have their Genitive Plural in **-ium.**

(*d*) Note the following nouns:

mel-**mellis** (n), *honey*	aes-**aeris** (n), *bronze*
iter-**itineris** (n), *journey*	genus-**generis** (n), *race, kind*
carō-**carnis** (f), *flesh*	tellūs-**tellūris** (f), *land*
trabs-**trabis** (f), *beam*	seges-**segetis** (f), *crop*
lac-**lactis** (n), *milk*	cor-**cordis** (n), *heart*
pecus-**pecudis** (f), *beast*	pecus-**pecoris** (n), *herd*
supellex-**supellectilis** (f), *furniture*	fur-**furis** (m), *thief*
rūs-**rūris** (n), *country*	plēbs-**plēbis** (f), *common people*
nix-**nivis** (f), *snow*	palūs-**palūdis** (f), *marsh*

(*e*) In poetry the **Accusative Plural** of Third Declension Nouns and Adjectives with Genitive Plural in **-ium** is often written as **-īs**, e.g. omnīs, fontīs.

47. *Fourth Declension*
The following Nouns have their **Dative** and **Ablative Plural** in **-ubus**:

acus-ūs (f),	*needle*	
arcus-ūs (m),	*bow*	
quercus-ūs (f),	*oak*	
tribus-ūs (f),	*tribe*	

But, **lacus-ūs** (m), *lake* and **portus-ūs** (m) *harbour* have both **-ibus** and **-ubus.**

48. *Fifth Declension*

(*a*) Only **diēs** and **rēs** have a complete Plural.

(*b*) **Aciēs-aciēī** (f), *line of battle* and **spēs-speī** (f), *hope* have Nominative and Accusative Plural.

(*c*) The following Nouns have no Plural.

> merīdiēs–diēī (m),   *midday*
> fidēs–eī (f),   *faith*
> plēbēs–eī (f),   *common people*

(*d*) **Diēs** is **Feminine** when it means *length of time* or *appointed day*, e.g. diē cōnstitūtā, *on a fixed day.*

(*e*) **Rēspūblica – reīpūblicae** (f), *state*, declines thus:

	SINGULAR	PLURAL
Nom.	rēspūblica	rēspūblicae
Acc.	rempūblicam	rēspūblicās
Gen.	reīpūblicae	rērumpūblicārum
Dat.	reīpūblicae	rēbuspūblicīs
Abl.	rēpūblicā	rēbuspūblicīs

49. The following nouns are found only in the **Plural:**

> **angustiae – ārum** (f), *narrow pass*
> **arma – ōrum** (n),   *arms*
> **dīvitiae – ārum** (f),   *wealth*
> **excubiae – ārum** (f),   *watch*
> **fēriae – ārum** (f),   *holidays*
> **hīberna – ōrum** (n),   *winter quarters*
> **Kalendae – ārum** (f), *Kalends*
> **Idūs – uum** (f),   *Ides*
> **īnsidiae – ārum** (f),   *ambush*
> **līberī – ōrum** (m),   *children*
> **minae – ārum** (f),   *threats*
> **maiōrēs – um** (m),   *ancestors*
> **moenia – ium** (n),   *city walls*
> **Nōnae – ārum** (f),   *Nones*
> **spolia – ōrum** (n),   *spoils*
> **tenebrae – ārum** (f), *darkness*

50. The following nouns change their meaning in the **Plural**:

NOUN	SINGULAR	PLURAL
aedēs – is (f)	*temple*	*house*
auxilium – iī (n)	*help*	*auxiliary forces*
castrum – ī (n)	*fort*	*camp*
cōpia – ae (f)	*supply*	*forces*
fīnis – is (m)	*end*	*territory*
fortūna – ae (f)	*chance, fortune*	*wealth*
grātia – ae (f)	*favour*	*thanks*
impedīmentum – ī (n)	*hindrance*	*heavy baggage*
littera – ae (f)	*letter of alphabet*	*letter, dispatch, literature*
mōs – mōris (m)	*custom*	*character*
opem (f)	*help*	*resources*
pars – partis (f)	*part*	*political party*
rōstrum – ī (n)	*beak, prow*	*speaker's platform*
vīs (f)	*violence*	*strength*

51. The following nouns are indeclinable:

fās, *right, divine law*
nefās, *sin*
$\left\{ \begin{array}{l} \textbf{nihil} \\ \textbf{nil} \end{array} \right\}$, *nothing*

52. In poetry Greek proper names such as **Aeneas** or **Anchises** are declined as follows:

Nom.	Aenēās	Anchīsēs
Voc.	Aenēā	Anchīsē (ā)
Acc.	Aenēān (am)	Anchīsēn (am)
Gen.	Aenēae	Anchīsae
Dat.	Aenēae	Anchīsae
Abl.	Aenēā	Anchīsā

IX. ADJECTIVES AND ADVERBS

53. **Uter,** *which of two,* agrees with a **Noun,** but takes the **Genitive** of a **Personal Pronoun.**

> e.g. Uter servus? *Which of the two slaves?*
> **but** Uter vestr**um**? *Which of you?*

54. In poetry **Third Declension Adjectives** and **Present Participles** often have their **Genitive Plural** in **-um.**

> e.g. ingent**um,** audient**um**

55. particeps – participis, *sharing in* ⎫ have their **Ablative Singular**
    superstes – superstitis, *surviving* ⎬ in **-e** and their **Genitive Plural**
    sospes – sospitis, *safe* ⎭ in **-um**

    inops – inopis, *in need* ⎫ have their **Genitive Plural** in **-um**
    memor – memoris, *mindful* ⎭

56. *Comparison of Adjectives*
    (*a*) In addition to the Adjectives listed in sec. 20 (*d*) the following are also irregular in Comparison:

POSITIVE	COMPARATIVE	SUPERLATIVE	
benevolus	benevol**entior**	benevol**entissimus**	*kind*
magnificus	magnific**entior**	magnific**entissimus**	*noble*
dīves	⎧ dīvit**ior** ⎩ dītior	dīvit**issimus** ⎫ dīt**issimus** ⎭	*rich*
pius	**magis** pius	**maximē** pius	*pious*
vetus	vetus**tior**	veter**rimus**	*old*
iuvenis	⎧ iū**nior** ⎫ ⎩ **minor nātū** ⎭	**minimus nātū**	*young*
senex	⎧ sen**ior** ⎫ ⎩ **māior nātū** ⎭	**maximus nātū**	*old*

(*b*) The following Adjectives either have no Positive or it is rarely found.

COMPARATIVE	SUPERLATIVE
exter**ior**, *outer*	extrē**mus**, *outmost, furthest*
inter**ior**, *inner*	int**imus**, *inmost*
īnfer**ior**, *lower*	{īnf**imus**, *lowest* / **imus**, *bottom of*
super**ior**, *higher*	{suprē**mus**, *final* / **summus**, *top of*
poster**ior**, *later*	postrē**mus**, *last*
pr**ior**, *former*	prī**mus**, *first*
prop**ior**, *nearer*	prox**imus**, *nearest*
ulter**ior**, *further*	ult**imus**, *furthest, last*

(*c*) **Plūrēs**, *more* and **complūrēs**, *several* have their **Genitive Plural** in -**ium**.

57. *Further Comparison of Adverbs*

POSITIVE	COMPARATIVE	SUPERLATIVE	
citō	cit**ius**	cit**issimē**	*quickly*
nūper	—	nūper**rimē**	*recently*
—	prius, {*before* / *sooner*	prīm**um** / prīm**ō**	*firstly* / *at first*

58. The following groups contain some common Adverbs.

-am ADVERBS

clam, *secretly*
pal**am**, *openly*
cōr**am**, *in the presence of*

-e ADVERBS

ferē, *almost*
repente, *suddenly*
valdē, *exceedingly*

forte, *by chance*
sponte, *willingly*
temere, *at random, rashly*

-em ADVERBS

salt**em**, *at least*
it**em**, *likewise*

-o ADVERBS

meritō, *deservedly*
crēbrō, *frequently*
subitō, *suddenly*
sērō, *late, too late*
tūtō, *in safety*
ultrō, *voluntarily*
cōnsultō, *on purpose*
falsō, *falsely*
continuō, *forthwith*
praestō, *at hand*

-im ADVERBS

gradā**tim**, *step by step*
paulā**tim**, *little by little*
pedetemp**tim**, *gradually*
inter**im**, *meanwhile*
praeser**tim**, *especially*
fūr**tim**, *stealthily*
pas**sim**, *here and there*

59. The **Accusative Singular Neuter** of many Adjectives is used as an **Adverb.**

mult**um**, *much*	nimi**um**, *too much*
paul**um**, *a little*	cēter**um**, *for the rest*
aliquant**um**, *somewhat*	prīm**um**, *firstly*
par**um**, *too little*	postrēm**um**, *finally*

60. *Table of Adverbs of Place*

	REST	TO	FROM
here	hīc	hūc	hinc
there	ibī	eō	inde
where	ubī	quō	unde

N.B. All Adverbs meaning *here* begin with the letter **h.**

X. PRONOUNS

61. (*a*) The suffix **-met** may be added for emphasis to all parts of **ego** except **nostrum,** to all parts of **tū** except **tū** and **vestrum,** to **sē** and **sibi,** e.g. mēmet, tibimet, sēmet.

(*b*) The form **sēsē** is found for **sē.**

(*c*) **iī** is found for **eī, iīs** for **eīs,** and **īsdem** for **eīsdem.**

62. (*a*) **Iste – ista – istud,** *that of yours,* declines like **ille.**

(*b*) The following Pronouns decline like **quī – quae – quod.**

quīvīs – quaevīs – quodvīs   ⎫
quīlibet – quaelibet – quodlibet ⎬ *any you like, any one at all*
   ⎭
quīnam – quaenam – quodnam, *which, please?*
aliquī – aliqua – aliquod, *some*

(*c*) The following Pronouns decline like **quis – quis – quid.**

quispiam – quaepiam – quidpiam, *someone*
quisnam – quisnam – quidnam, *who please?*

(*d*) **Quis, quī** after **nē, num, sī, nisi** mean *anyone, any* and usually have **qua** as (i) the Nominative Feminine Singular and (ii) the Nominative and Accusative Neuter Plural.

e.g. sī **quis,** *if anyone;* sī **qua** legiō, *if any legion.*

(*e*) **Quī** is an old form of the **Ablative Singular** of **quī.**
Quīs is an old form of the **Dative** and **Ablative Plural** of
quī.

(*f*) **Quisque,** *each,* is written immediately after a **Numeral
Adjective,** a **Superlative Adjective** and **suus.**

> e.g. Fortissimus **quisque,** *all the bravest men*
> Decimō **quōque** annō, *every tenth year*
> Librum suum **quisque** legēbat, *each one was reading his own
> book*

XI. VERBS

63. As well as the Present Imperative the Latin Verb has a
Future Imperative which is sometimes used for emphasis.
It is remarkable in that it has a **Third Person.**

ACTIVE

(*a*)	FIRST	SECOND	THIRD	FOURTH
Singular	amātō	monētō	regitō	audītō
	amātō	monētō	regitō	audītō
Plural	amātōte	monētōte	regitōte	audītōte
	amantō	monentō	reguntō	audiuntō

PASSIVE

Singular	amātor	monētor	regitor	audītor
	amātor	monētor	regitor	audītor
	—	—	—	—
Plural	amantor	monentor	reguntor	audiuntor

(*b*) The Future Imperative of **sum.**

	Singular		Plural	
	estō		**estōte**	
	estō		**suntō**	

(*c*) The following Verbs have a contracted **Singular** Imperative.

> dīcō has **dīc**
> dūcō has **dūc**
> faciō has **fac**
> ferō has **fer**

N.B. Their Plurals are regular, dī**cite,** dū**cite,** fa**cite,** fer**te.**

64. *Declension of the Gerund*

Nom.	(am**āre**)
Acc.	(am**āre**), ad am**andum**
Gen.	am**andī**
Dat.	am**andō**
Abl.	am**andō**

65. The Latin Verb has a **Second Supine** ending in **-u**, used in such phrases as,

facile dict**ū**, difficile fact**ū**, *easy to say, difficult to do*
mīrābile vīs**ū**, *amazing to see*

66. The Latin Verb has certain **Contracted Endings.**
(*a*) Second Person Singular Future and Imperfect Indicative Passive

e.g. amābe**re** for amāberis
    capiē**re** for capiēris
    regēbā**re** for regēbāris

(*b*) Second Person Singular Present and Imperfect Subjunctive Passive

e.g. moneā**re** for moneāris
    audīrē**re** for audīrēris

(*c*) Second Person Singular and Plural Perfect Indicative Active

e.g. amā**stī** for amāvistī
    dēlē**stis** for dēlēvistis

(*d*) Third Person Plural Perfect Indicative Active

e.g. amāvē**re** for amāvērunt
    rēxē**re** for rēxērunt

(e) Perfect Infinitive Active

> e.g. laud**āsse** for laudāvisse
> aud**isse** for audivisse

N.B. (c) (e) only occur in Verbs which have a **-v** in their **Perfect Stem.**

(f) In the Fourth Conjugation the **-v** of the **Perfect Stem** is often omitted.

> e.g. audi**erim** for audiverim
> sci**it** for scivit

67. *Defective Verbs*

> **ōdī,** *I hate*
> **meminī,** *I remember* } are found only in the **Perfect** tenses.
> **nōvī,** *I know*

Observe the rule,
> Latin Perfect = English Present
> Latin Pluperfect = English Past
> Latin Future Perfect = English Future

ōdī, *I hate*	**meminī,** *I remember*	**nōvī,** *I know*
ōderam, *I hated*	**memineram,** *I remembered*	**nōveram,** *I knew*
ōderō, *I shall hate*	**meminerō,** *I shall remember*	**nōverō,** *I shall know*
	ōdisse, *to hate*	
	meminisse, *to remember*	
	nōvisse, *to know*	

Similarly with the Subjunctive Mood

> **ōderim**
> **meminerim** } = Present Subjunctive
> **nōverim**
> **ōdissem**
> **meminissem** } = Imperfect or Past Subjunctive
> **nōvissem**

N.B. The Imperative of **memini** is **mementō**
                                      mementōte

XII. NUMBERS

68.

	DISTRIBUTIVES (*one each*, etc.)	ADVERBS (*once, twice*, etc.)
1	singulī-**ae-a**	semel
2	bīnī	bis
3	ternī, trīnī	ter
4	quaternī	quater
5	quīnī	quīnqui**ēs**
6	sēnī	sexi**ēs**
7	septēnī	septi**ēs**
8	octōnī	octi**ēs**
9	novēnī	novi**ēs**
10	dēnī	deci**ēs**
11	ūndēnī	ūndeci**ēs**
12	duodēnī	duodeci**ēs**
13	ternī dēnī	terdeci**ēs**
14	quaternī dēnī	quater deci**ēs**
15	quīnī dēni	quīndeci**ēs**
16	sēnī dēnī	sēdeci**ēs**
17	septēnī dēnī	septi**ēs** deci**ēs**
18	duodēvīcēnī	duodēvīci**ēs**
19	ūndēvīcēnī	ūndēvīci**ēs**
20	vīcēnī	vīci**ēs**
30	trīcēnī	trīci**ēs**
40	quadrāgēnī	quadrāgi**ēs**
50	quīnquāgēnī	quīnquāgi**ēs**
60	sexāgēnī	sexāgi**ēs**
70	septuāgēnī	septuāgi**ēs**
80	octōgēnī	octōgi**ēs**
90	nōnāgēnī	nōnāgi**ēs**
100	centēnī	centi**ēs**
200	ducēnī	ducenti**ēs**
300	trecēnī	trecenti**ēs**
400	quadringēnī	quadringenti**ēs**
500	quīngēnī	quīngenti**ēs**
600	sēscēnī	sescenti**ēs**

700	septingēnī	septingentiēs
800	octingēnī	octingentiēs
900	nōngēnī	nōngentiēs
1000	singula mīlia	mīliēs

N.B. **(i)** Distinguish the use of the **Cardinal** and **Distributive**.

e.g. **Tria** māla puerīs dedit, *he gave the boys three apples.*
Terna māla puerīs dedit, *he gave the boys three apples each.*

(ii) Distributives are used instead of Cardinals with Nouns **Plural** in form but **Singular** in meaning.

e.g. **Bīna** castra, *two camps*
Bis **bīna** sunt quattuor, *2 × 2 = 4*
Trīnae litterae, *three letters*

(iii) Fractions of the type $\dfrac{n-1}{n}$ are expressed thus,

sex partēs $= \frac{6}{7}$

trēs partēs $= \frac{3}{4}$

(iv) 1,000,000 is **deciēs centēna mīlia,** i.e. 10 × 100,000
Centēna mīlia is often omitted especially in sums of money.

e.g. Vīciēs sēstertium = vīciēs **centēna mīlia** sēstertium
$= 20 × 100,000$
$= 2,000,000$ *sesterces*

(v) prīmum, *for the first time*
iterum, *for the second time*
postrēmum, *for the last time*

In arguments, prīmum, *firstly*
deinde, *secondly*
$\left.\begin{matrix} \text{postrēmo} \\ \text{dēnique} \end{matrix}\right\}$, *finally*

Essential Syntax

XIII. NOUNS

69. *Nominative Case*

The Nominative is used to indicate the **Subject** of the Verb.

e.g. **Puer** pilam iacit. *The boy throws the ball.*

70. *Vocative Case*

The Vocative is used **to address** a person and always has the **same** ending as the Nominative except in the Singular of **-us** and **-ius Nouns of the Second Declension.**

e.g. Festīnā domum, **serve.** *Hurry home, slave.*

71. *Accusative Case*

(*a*) The Accusative is used to indicate the **Direct Object** of the Verb.

e.g. Mīles **hastam** tenet. *The soldier holds his spear.*

(*b*) The Accusative is used in **Exclamations.**

e.g. O **mē miserum!** *Dear me!*
Quantam impudentiam! *What great impudence!*

(*c*) The Accusative Neuter Singular of an **Adjective** or a **Pronoun** may be used as an **Adverb.**

e.g. **Nihil** assentior. *I do not agree at all* (lit. *in no way do I agree*).
Quid erravērunt? *In what respect have they erred?*

72. *Genitive Case*

(*a*) The Genitive is used to indicate **Possession.**

e.g. Mīlitēs **rēgis** victī sunt. *The* $\left\{\begin{array}{l}\textit{soldiers of the king}\\\textit{king's soldiers}\end{array}\right\}$ *were defeated.*

(*b*) The Genitive is used to indicate that only a **Part** or **Some** of the whole is involved, after a **Neuter Adjective, Pronoun** or **Adverb.**

e.g.

nihil		*no*	
aliquid		*some*	
nimis		*too much*	
parum		*too little*	
satis	**pecūniae**	*enough*	*money*
plūs		*more*	
minus		*less*	
tantum		*so much*	
quantum		*how much*	

N.B. Nostrum and **vestrum** are the Genitive Plurals of **ego** and **tū** which indicate **some** or **part.**

e.g. Quis **vestrum**? *Who of you?*
but Omnēs **nōs**. *All of us.*

(*c*) The Genitive is used, always with an **Adjective,** to indicate an **Internal Quality.**

e.g. Fēmina **magnae virtūtis.** *A woman of great courage.*

The Genitive tends to be used for internal or permanent qualities, the Ablative for external ones, vid. sec. 74 (*e*).

(*d*) The Genitive is used to indicate **Value** after, **aestimō, habeō, dūcō, faciō,** *value.*

There are twelve common expressions of **Value.**

magnī, *greatly*	**plūris**	**plūrimī**
parvī, *at a little*	**minōris**	**minimī**
tantī, *at so much*	**quantī**	**tantulī,** *at so little*
nihilī, *at nothing*	**naucī,** *at a nut*	**floccī,** *at a straw*

e.g. Librōs **plūris** quam dīvitiās aestimābat. *He valued his books more highly than his wealth.*

Magnī mātrem habēbās. *You cared a lot for your mother.*

Floccī magistrum nōn facimus. *We do not care a straw for the teacher.*

(*e*) **Tantī, quantī, plūris, minōris** are used with the verbs **emō,** *buy* and **vendō,** *sell* to express **Price.** Vid. sec. 74 (*f*)

e.g. **Quantī** domum ēmistī? $\begin{cases} \textit{How much did you pay for the house?} \\ \textit{What did the house cost you?} \end{cases}$

(*f*) The Genitive is used after the following Adjectives.

cupidus, *desirous of*	**perītus,** *skilled in*
avidus, *eager for*	**imperītus,** *unskilled in*
studiōsus, *devoted to*	**īnsuētus,** *unaccustomed to*
memor, *mindful of*	**expers,** *without a share in*
immemor, *heedless of*	**particeps,** *sharing in*
similis, *like*	**dissimilis,** *unlike*

Also the Present Participles

amāns, *devoted to*	**patiēns,** *enduring of, inured to*

(*g*) The Genitive is used with the Verbs, **accūsō,** *accuse,* **damnō,** *condemn,* **absolvō,** *acquit* to indicate the **Charge** or **Punishment.**

e.g. **Perfidiae** accūsātus est. *He was accused of treachery.*

Nōs **capitis** damnābunt. *They will condemn us to death.*

73. *Dative Case*

(*a*) The Dative is used to indicate the **Indirect Object** of the Verb, often shown in English by **to** and **for.**

e.g. Gladium **mihi** dedit. *He gave the sword **to** me.*

(*b*) The Dative can indicate **Possession.**

e.g. **Nōbīs** canis est. *We have a dog.*

(*c*) The Dative can indicate **Purpose** and is followed by a second Dative of the **Person** or **Thing.** It is known as a **Predicative Dative.**

auxiliō esse, *to help*

auxiliō venīre, *to come to the help of*

auxiliō mittere, *to send to the help of*

beneficiō esse, *to be of advantage to*

ūsuī esse, *to be of use to*

dēdecorī esse, *to be a disgrace to*

praesidiō esse, *to guard*

odiō esse, *to be hated by*

impedīmentō esse, *to be a hindrance to*

exemplō esse, *to be an example*

e.g. Equitēs **peditibus auxiliō** mīsērunt. *They sent the cavalry to the help of the infantry.*

Odiō eīs eram. *I was hated by them.*

(*d*) The Dative is used after the following Adjectives

benignus, *kind*	**necessārius,** *necessary*
difficilis, *difficult*	**ūtilis,** *useful*
facilis, *easy*	**inūtilis,** *useless*
grātus, *pleasing*	**par,** *equal to*
idōneus, *suitable*	**impar,** *unequal*

74. *Ablative Case*

(*a*) The Ablative is used with **ā(b)** after a Passive Verb to indicate the **Agent.**

e.g. **Ā magistrō** laudātus sum. *I was praised by the teacher.*

(*b*) The Ablative is used **without** a preposition after an Active or Passive Verb to indicate the **Instrument** used.

e.g. **Hastā** vulnerātus est. *He was wounded by a spear.*

(*c*) The Ablative is used to indicate **How** an action is performed.

e.g. **Summā** cum **celeritāte** Rōmam vēnērunt. *They came to Rome with all speed.*

N.B. If there is no **Adjective** present, **cum** is generally used. If there is an **Adjective** present, **cum** is optional.

e.g. **cum** cūrā. *With care.*

magnā (**cum**) cūrā. *With great care.*

(*d*) The Ablative is used **without** a preposition to indicate **Why** an action takes place.

c

e.g. **Fame** periērunt. *They died of hunger.*

Mīles **ignāviā** damnātus est. *The soldier was condemned because of his cowardice.*

(*e*) The Ablative is used with an **Adjective** to describe an **External** or **Physical Feature**, vid. sec. 72 (*c*).

e.g. Vir **nigrā barbā**. *A man with a black beard.*

Nāvis **altō mālō**. *A ship with a high mast.*

(*f*) The Ablative is used after the Verbs, **emō**, *buy* and **vendō**, *sell* to express **Price**, vid. sec. 72 (*e*).

e.g. **Duōbus mīlibus** sēstertium domum ēmit. *He bought the house for two thousand sesterces.*

Vīlī equum vendidit. *He sold the horse cheaply.*

(*g*) The Ablative can be used after a **Comparative** to replace **quam** with a **Nominative** or **Accusative**.

e.g. Tu fortior **mē** es. *You are braver than I.*

(*h*) The Ablative is used after the following **Adjectives**.

dignus, *worthy of*	**frētus**, *relying on*
indignus, *unworthy of*	**praeditus**, *endowed with*
contentus, *content with*	**ortus**, *descended from*
orbus, *bereft of*	**vacuus**, *empty of*

XIV. ADJECTIVES

75. (*a*) An Adjective tells us something about a Noun or Pronoun and so agrees with it in **Case, Number** and **Gender**.

e.g. Pōns **maximus** factus est. *A very large bridge was built.*

Puellae erant **pulchrae**. *The girls were beautiful.*

In urbe **parvā**. *In a small city.*

(*b*) If an Adjective describes persons of different sex, it generally becomes **Masculine** and **Plural**.

e.g. Puer et puella **bonī** sunt. *The boy and girl are good.*

(*c*) If an Adjective describes things of different gender, it generally becomes **Neuter** and **Plural**.

e.g. Domus et templum erant **pulchra**. *The house and temple were beautiful.*

N.B. In (*b*) and (*c*) the Adjective may agree with the **nearest** Noun.

> e.g. Laudā**tus** est pater et māter. *My father and mother were praised.*

76. The English Nouns, *top of, bottom of,* etc. are replaced by **Adjectives** in Latin.

> **summus,** *top of*   **reliquus,** *rest of*
> **medius,** *middle of*   **tōtus,** *whole of*
> **īmus,** *bottom of*   **extrēmus,** *edge of*
>   **cēterī,** *the rest of*

> e.g. Ad **summum** collem pervēnit. *He reached the top of the hill.*
> Cum **reliquō** exercitū prōgressus est. *He advanced with the rest of the army.*

XV. PRONOUNS

77. *Personal Pronouns*

(*a*) *I, you,* etc. are normally not expressed in Latin but indicated by the **ending** of the Verb. **Ego, tū,** etc. are used for **emphasis.**

> e.g. **Ego** rūs īvī, **tū** domī manēbās. *I went to the country, you stayed at home.*

(*b*) Latin is not a polite language: **ego** is written before **tū,** and **tū** before **is.**

> e.g. **Ego** et **tū** aderāmus. *You and I were present.*
> **Tū** et **is** ā magistrō culpātī estis. *He and you were blamed by the teacher.*

N.B. A **First and Second Person Subject** makes the Verb **First Plural.**

A **Second and Third Person Subject** makes the Verb **Second Plural.**

78. *Relative Pronouns.*

The Relative agrees with its **Antecedent** in **Number, Person** and **Gender,** but its **Case** is decided by its **position** in its **own clause.**

e.g. Linter **quam** vīdimus est vestra. *The boat which we saw is yours.*

Puella **cūius** pila āmissa erat flēbat. *The girl whose ball had been lost was weeping.*

Vōs, **quī** adestis, gaudēre dēbētis. *You who are here should rejoice.*

XVI. COMPARATIVES AND SUPERLATIVES

79. *Comparatives*

(*a*) When comparing one person or thing with another, Latin uses the word **quam** with the same case **after** it as **before** it.

e.g. Poēta est māior **quam** agricola. *The poet is bigger than the farmer.*

Puellam stultiōrem **quam** puerum vocāvit. *He called the girl more stupid than the boy.*

N.B. Quam with a **Nominative** or **Accusative** may be replaced by the **Ablative,** vid. sec. 74 (*g*).

(*b*) If two Adjectives are compared, **both** must be **Comparatives.**

e.g. Mīles est stultior quam **īgnāvior.** *The soldier is more stupid than lazy.*

(*c*) In English a phrase such as **that of** frequently occurs after a Comparative, in Latin it is **not** translated.

e.g. Meus canis est māior quam **Publiī.** *My dog is bigger than that of Publius.*

(*d*) **Quam** is omitted after **plūs, amplius** and **minus.**

e.g. **Plūs** septuāgintā mīlitēs occīsī sunt. *More than seventy soldiers were killed.*

(*e*) The Comparative can also have the meanings, *rather, too, quite.*

e.g. Ille est pulchrior. *That man is* $\begin{cases} rather \\ quite \\ too \end{cases}$ *handsome.*

80. *Superlatives*

(*a*) The Superlatives can also have the meanings, *very, extremely.*

e.g. Puella erat tardissima. *The girl was* $\begin{Bmatrix} very \\ extremely \end{Bmatrix}$ *slow.*

(*b*) **Quam** with the Superlative means, *as . . . as possible.*

e.g. **Quam celerrimē** cucurrērunt. *They ran as quickly as possible.*

(*c*) The Superlative is often used with a person's name thus,
Caesar vir **fortissimus.** *The brave Caesar.*

XVII. VERBS

81. *Present Tense*

(*a*) The Present denotes what is going on **now** or what **is.**

e.g. Canis **currit.** *The dog runs, is running, does run.*
Canis **est** ferōx. *The dog is fierce.*

(*b*) The Present denotes an action begun in the **past** and still going on **now,** usually with the Adverbs **iam, iam diū, dūdum, prīdem.**

e.g. Trēs iam hōrās **adsum.** *I have been here for three hours (and still am here).*

Iam $\begin{Bmatrix} diū \\ dūdum \\ prīdem \end{Bmatrix}$ in murō **sedeō.** *I have long been sitting on the wall (and still am sitting).*

(*c*) The Present is frequently used in Latin instead of the Perfect to make a narrative more vivid and exciting for the reader.

e.g. Metellus ab Zamā **discēdit,** et in hīs urbibus, quae ad sē dēfēcerant, praesidia **impōnit;** cēterum exercitum in Numidiā **collocat.**

Metellus left Zama and put garrisons in those towns which had revolted to him; the rest of the army he stationed in Numidia.

82. *Future Tense*

The Future denotes what is **going** to happen or what will **be.**

> e.g. Ad tē **scrībam.** *I shall write to you.*
> Epistula longa **erit.** *The letter will be long.*

83. *Imperfect Tense*

(*a*) The Imperfect denotes what **went on** or what **was for a long time.**

> e.g. Puer **lacrimābat** et īnfēlīx **erat.** *The boy was crying and was unhappy.*

(*b*) The Imperfect denotes a **repeated action** in the **past.**

> e.g. Prīmā lūce **surgēbat.** *He used to get up at dawn.*

(*c*) The Imperfect denotes an **attempted action** in the **past.**

> e.g. Puer arborem **ascendēbat.** *The boy tried to climb the tree.*

(*d*) The Imperfect denotes an action begun in the **past** and **still continuing** at the time mentioned, usually with Adverbs, **iam, iam diū, dūdum, pridem**

> e.g. Trēs iam hōrās **aderam.** *I had been present for three hours (and still was present).*
>
> Iam $\begin{cases} \text{diū} \\ \text{dūdum} \\ \text{pridem} \end{cases}$ in murō **sedēbam.** *I had long been sitting on the (wall and still was sitting).*

84. *Perfect Tense*

(*a*) The Perfect denotes a **'once'** action in the past, i.e. without **have.**

> e.g. **Vēnī, vīdī, vīcī.** *I came, I saw, I conquered.*

(*b*) The Perfect denotes the **present** result of a **past** action, i.e. with **have.**

> e.g. Pontem **fēcērunt.** *They have built the bridge.*

85. *Future Perfect Tense*

The Future Perfect denotes an action which will take place **before** another action in the **future.** In Latin it occurs most commonly in **Subordinate Clauses** where English uses a Present.

> e.g. Sī **redieris,** poenās dabis. *If you return, you will be punished.*
> Cum Rōmam **vēnerit,** Cicerōnem audiet. *When he comes to Rome, he will listen to Cicero.*

86. *Pluperfect Tense*

The Pluperfect denotes an action already completed **before** another action in the **past.**

> e.g. Rēgem **occīderant** priusquam pervēnimus. *They had killed the king before we arrived.*

87. *The Infinitive*

The Infinitive which is really a **Noun** can act as **Subject** or **Object.**

(*a*) As Subject

> e.g. **Natāre** est facile. $\left\{ \begin{array}{l} \textit{To swim} \\ \textit{Swimming} \end{array} \right\}$ *is easy.*

(*b*) As Object

> e.g. Latīnē **scrībere** possum. *I can write Latin.*
> **Natāre** sciō. *I know how to swim.*

N.B. The following Verbs take the Infinitive as Object.

volō, *wish, be willing*	**prohibeō,** *prevent*
nōlō, *be unwilling*	**audeō,** *dare*
mālō, *prefer*	**cōnor,** *try*
possum, *be able, can*	**dēsinō,** *cease*
dēbeō, *ought*	$\left. \begin{array}{l} \textbf{dubitō} \\ \textbf{cūnctor} \end{array} \right\}$ *hesitate*
$\left. \begin{array}{l} \textbf{statuō} \\ \textbf{cōnstituō} \end{array} \right\}$ *decide*	
cupiō, *desire*	**soleō,** *be accustomed to*
sinō, *allow*	**sciō,** *know*
cōgō, *compel*	**coepī,** *began*

N.B. (i) Possum, dēbeō are **never** followed by a Perfect Infinitive as in English.

e.g. **Venīre** $\begin{cases} \text{poterat.} \\ \text{dēbuit.} \end{cases}$ *He* $\begin{cases} \textit{could have come.} \\ \textit{ought to have come.} \end{cases}$

(ii) Coepī if followed by a **Passive Infinitive** becomes **Passive** itself.

e.g. Urbs oppugnārī **coepta est.** *The city began to be attacked.*

(c) In Latin the **Present Infinitive** can be used instead of a **Perfect Indicative** to denote a quick moving vivid narrative and is known as the **Historic Infinitive.**

e.g. Verrēs **minitārī** eī, **vōciferārī,** lacrimās interdum vix **tenēre.**
Verres uttered threats against him, shouted aloud, at times could hardly restrain his tears.

88. *Participles*

Present Participle

(a) The Present Participle denotes an action going on at the **same time** as the **Main Verb** and is often equivalent to a **'while'** clause.

e.g. **Rediēns** domum, lupum vīdit.
$\begin{cases} \textit{Returning home} \\ \textit{While he was returning home} \end{cases}$ *he saw a wolf.*
Puerōs **aufugientēs** animadvertit.
He noticed the boys $\begin{cases} \textit{running away.} \\ \textit{while they were running away.} \end{cases}$

(b) In Latin a Present Participle is not used in the **Nominative Case** if there is any suggestion of **Cause, cum** is used with a **Present** or **Imperfect Subjunctive.**

e.g. **Cum** magistrum **timēret,** puer tacēbat.
$\begin{cases} \textit{Fearing the teacher} \\ \textit{Since he feared the teacher} \end{cases}$ *the boy kept silent.*

(c) A Present Participle can be used to translate such **Nouns** as, *audience, bystanders,* etc.

e.g. Clāmōrēs **audientium.** *The shouts of the audience.*
Adstantēs vītāvit. *He avoided the bystanders.*

N.B. In Latin a Present Participle by **itself** can often be translated by a **Relative Clause**.

e.g. **Pugnantēs** spectābam. *I watched those who were fighting.*

89. *Perfect Participle*

(*a*) The Perfect Participle denotes an action finished **before** that of the **Main Verb**.

e.g. Puerī **laudātī** ā cōnsule gaudēbant.

The boys $\begin{cases} having\ been\ praised \\ praised \end{cases}$ *by the consul were happy.*

(*b*) The Perfect Participle of Deponent Verb is **Active** in meaning.

e.g. **Regressī** ad castra cubitum īvērunt.

$\begin{cases} Having\ returned \\ Returning \end{cases}$ *to the camp they went to bed.*

N.B. English often uses a Present Participle to denote an action finished **before** that of the Main Verb, but Latin being more precise uses the correct Participle, the **Perfect.**

(*c*) Latin often uses a **Perfect Participle** in agreement with a **Noun** in the **Accusative Case** and **one** Main Verb where English uses two Verbs joined by **and**.

e.g. Faelis mūrem **captum** ēdit. *The cat caught the mouse and ate it.*

(*d*) For Ablative Absolute vid. sec. 103.

90. *Future Participle*

(*a*) The Future Participle denotes an action that is **about to** or **going to take place**.

e.g. Arborem **cāsūram** spectābam.

I watched the tree $\begin{cases} about\ to\ fall. \\ going\ to\ fall. \\ on\ the\ point\ of\ falling. \end{cases}$

(*b*) The Future Participle is often used with **sum** or **eram** to denote **intention** or **likelihood**.

e.g. **Reditūrī** sunt. *They are* $\begin{cases} going\ to \\ likely\ to \\ intending\ to \end{cases}$ *return.*

Discessūrī erant. *They were on the* $\begin{cases} point \\ verge \end{cases}$ *of leaving.*

91. In Latin the following Verbs put their **Object** into the **Dative.**

(*a*) FIRST CONJUGATION
imperō, *order*
appropinquō, *approach*
obtemperō, *obey*
vacō, *have leisure for*

SECOND CONJUGATION
displiceō, *displease*
faveō, *favour*
indulgeō, *indulge in*
invideō, *envy*
medeor, *heal*
noceō, *harm*
pāreō, *obey*
persuādeō, *persuade*
placeō, *please*
studeō, *study*
suādeō, *persuade*

THIRD CONJUGATION
cōnfīdō, fīdō, *trust*
cōnsulō, *consult the interest of.*
crēdō, *believe*
diffīdō, *distrust*
īgnōscō, *pardon*
īrāscor, *be angry with*
nūbō, *marry*
obsistō, obstō, *obstruct*
occurrō, *meet*
parcō, *spare*
resistō, *resist*
serviō, *serve, play the slave to*
subveniō, *help*
succurrō, *help*

N.B. **(i)** **crēdō** is followed by the **Dative** of **Person,** but **Accusative** of a **Neuter Pronoun** (to avoid ambiguity).

e.g. **Eī** crēdēbāmus. *We believed him.*
Id crēdēbāmus. *We believed that.*

(ii) **cōnsulō** + **Accusative** means *consult*
cōnsulō + **Dative** means *consult the interests of*
cōnsulō + **dē** + **Ablative** means *consult about*

(*b*) In the **Passive** these Verbs must be used **Impersonally,** i.e. **it** becomes the **Subject** and the English Subject goes into the **Dative.**

e.g. **Eī** crēditur. *He is believed.*
Tibi parsum est. *You were spared.*

92. In Latin the following Verbs put their **Objects** into the **Genitive**.

> **meminī,** *I remember*
> **oblīvīscor,** *I forget*
> **misereor,** *I pity*

N.B. meminī and **oblīvīscor** take the **Genitive** of **Person** and the **Accusative** or **Genitive** of **Thing,** but if the **Object** is a **Neuter Pronoun,** the **Accusative** must be used.

> e.g. **Tuī** meminī sed $\begin{cases} \textbf{tuum nōmen} \\ \textbf{tuī nōminis} \end{cases}$ oblīvīscor.
>
> *I remember you, but forget your name.*
> **But,** mementō **hōc.** *Remember this.*

93. In Latin the following Verbs put their **Objects** into the **Ablative**.

ūtor, *use*	**vescor,** *feed on*
abūtor, *use up*	**careō,** *lack* (usually a luxury)
fruor, *enjoy*	**egeō,** *need* (an essential)
fungor, *perform*	**opus est,** *there is need of*
potior, *gain control of*	

N.B. Opus est takes the **Dative** of **Subject, Ablative** of **Thing Needed.**

> e.g. **Tibi pecūniā** opus erit. *You will need money.*

94. In Latin there are numerous Verbs which are used **Impersonally,** i.e. the **Subject** is **it** and the Verb if Indicative or Subjunctive is always **Third Person Singular.**

(*a*) The following Verbs take the **Accusative** of **Person** and are followed by the **Present Infinitive.**

> **mē decet,** *it becomes me*
> **mē dēdecet,** *it ill becomes me*
> **mē oportet,** *it behoves me, I ought to*

N.B. Oportet can only be followed by a **Present Infinitive.**

> e.g. **Tē venīre** oportuit. *You should have come.*

(*b*) The following Verbs take the **Dative** of the **Subject** and are followed by a **Present Infinitive.**

> **mihi vidētur,** *it seems good to me, I am resolved*
> **mihi placet,** *it pleases me, I am resolved*
> **mihi licet,** *it is allowed to me, I may*
> **mihi libet,** *it pleases me, I like*

e.g. **Eī redīre** licuit. *He was allowed to return.*

(*c*) The following Verbs take the **Accusative** of the **Subject** and **Genitive** of the **Cause.**

> **mē miseret,** *I pity, feel sorry for*
> **mē paenitet,** *I repent of*
> **mē piget,** *I am vexed with*
> **mē pudet,** *I am ashamed of*
> **mē taedet,** *I am tired of*

e.g. **Nōs senis** miserēbat. *We felt sorry for the old man.*

N.B. (i) A **Prohibition** is expressed by **ne + Present Subjunctive.**

e.g. **Nē tē** meī **pudeat.** *Don't be ashamed of me.*

(ii) If the **Object** is a **Neuter Pronoun,** it goes into the **Nominative.**

e.g. **Hōc** mē paenitēbit. *I shall repent of this.*

(iii) These Verbs may be followed by an **Infinitive.**

e.g. **Discessisse** domō mē nōn paenitet. *I do not regret having left home.*

(Note that here, **discessisse** is really **Subject,** i.e. *To have left home does not repent me.*)

(*d*) Many **Intransitive Verbs** are used **Impersonally** in the **Passive.**

e.g. Concursum est. *There was a rush.*
> Ad Britanniam ventum est. *Britain was reached.*
> Diū ac ācriter pugnātum est. *There was a long and fierce battle.*

(*e*) **Interest,** *it is of importance to,* is followed by a **Genitive** of the **Person** except **meā, tuā, nostrā, vestrā.**

e.g. $\begin{Bmatrix} \textbf{Rōmānōrum} \\ \textbf{Nostrā} \end{Bmatrix}$ intererat. *It was of importance to* $\begin{cases} \textit{the Romans.} \\ \textit{us.} \end{cases}$

N.B. **(i) Interest** may be used with a **Genitive of Value,** an **Adverb,** or the **Neuter Singular** of an **Adjective** used as an **Adverb.**

e.g. $\left\{\begin{array}{l}\textbf{Magnī}\\\textbf{Magnopere}\\\textbf{Multum}\end{array}\right\}$ meā intererit. $\left\{\begin{array}{l}\textit{It will be of great importance}\\\textit{to me.}\end{array}\right.$

(ii) Interest may be followed by

- (*a*) **Plain Infinitive**
- (*b*) **Accusative and Infinitive**
- (*c*) **Explanatory ut + Subjunctive**
- (*d*) **Indirect Question**

e.g. Plūrimī interest $\left\{\begin{array}{l}\text{collem } \textbf{capere.}\\\textbf{eōs} \text{ collem } \textbf{capere.}\\\textbf{ut} \text{ collem } \textbf{capiant.}\end{array}\right.$

It is of the greatest importance $\left\{\begin{array}{l}\textit{to capture the hill.}\\\textit{that they should capture the hill.}\end{array}\right.$

Nostrā nōn interest **utrum canās necne.**
It is immaterial to us whether you sing or not.

(*f*) **Rēfert,** *it concerns, is of importance to,* is followed only by **meā, tuā, nostrā, vestrā.**

e.g. $\left\{\begin{array}{l}\text{Nōn}\\\text{Nihil}\end{array}\right\}$ **meā** rēfert. *It makes no difference to me.*

(*g*) Latin has a small group of impersonal **Weather Verbs.**

> **pluit,** *it rains*
> **ningit,** *it snows*
> **tonat,** *it thunders*
> **fulgurat,** *there is lightning*

95. *Gerund*

The Gerund is a **Verbal Noun** (vid. sec. 64) used as follows

(*a*) In the **Accusative** with **ad** to express **Purpose.**

e.g. **Ad dīripiendum** vēnērunt. *They came to plunder.*

(*b*) In the **Genitive** after another Noun and with **causa** to express **Purpose.**

e.g. Ars **canendī.** *The art of singing.*
Dīripiendī causa vēnērunt. *They came to plunder.*

(*c*) In the **Ablative** to express **Instrument** and with a **Preposition.**

> e.g. **In dormiendō** tempus terēbant. *They wasted time in sleeping.*
> **Audiendō** discēs. *You will learn by listening.*

96. *Gerundive*

The Gerundive is a **Verbal Adjective Passive** in meaning – i.e. *requiring to be* – and is used as follows.

(*a*) To replace the **Gerund** when it has an **Object.**

> e.g. Lēgātiōnibus **mittendīs.** *By sending embassies.*
> $\left.\begin{array}{l}\text{Ad urbem } \textbf{dīripiendam}\\ \text{Urbis } \textbf{dīripiendae } \text{causa.}\end{array}\right\}$ *To plunder the city.*

N.B. The Gerund is retained when
  (**i**) the Verb takes the **Dative**
  (**ii**) the **Object** is a **Neuter Pronoun**

(*b*) To express **Obligation,** i.e. English, *must, have to.* The Latin sentence is in the **Passive** with the **Agent** in the **Dative.**

> e.g. Puer **magistrō laudandus** est.
> Lit. *The boy is requiring to be praised by the teacher.*
> i.e. *The teacher must praise the boy.*
>
> Puellae **tibi monendae** erant.
> Lit. *The girls were requiring to be warned by you.*
> i.e. *You had to warn the girls.*

N.B. (i) The Gerundive is used **Impersonally** if the Verb is **Intransitive.**

(**ii**) The Gerundive is used **Impersonally** if the Verb takes the **Dative** and the **Agent** is expressed by **ā(b)** with the **Ablative.**

> e.g. Nōbīs **festīnandum** erit. *We shall have to hurry.*
> Cōnsulī **ā mīlitibus pārendum** est. *The soldiers must obey the consul.*

(*c*) In the **Accusative** after the Verb **cūrō,** *I have something done.*

> e.g. Caesar pontem **faciendum** in flūmine cūrāvit.
> *Caesar had a bridge built across the river.*

XVIII. TIME, PLACE AND SPACE

97. *Time*

(*a*) Time **How Long** goes into the **Accusative Case. No Preposition.** English indicates Time How Long by **for** or by simply stating the length of time.

> e.g. **Trēs mēnsēs** rēgnābat. *He ruled (for) three months.*

(*b*) **All other time phrases** go into the **Ablative Case. No Preposition.** English uses such Prepositions as **in, within, at, on, during.**

> e.g. $\left\{\begin{array}{l}\textbf{Tribus diēbus} \\ \textbf{Prīmā lūce} \\ \textbf{Tertiō diē} \\ \textbf{Aestāte}\end{array}\right\}$ redībunt. *They will return* $\left\{\begin{array}{l}\textit{in three days.} \\ \textit{at dawn.} \\ \textit{on the third day.} \\ \textit{during the summer.}\end{array}\right.$

N.B. decem ante annīs.   *Ten years before.*
    decem post annīs.   *Ten years after.*
    abhinc annōs decem.   *Ten years ago.*

98. *Place*

(*a*) **To, from, in** a place are expressed by the Prepositions **ad, ē(x), ā(b), in** except with names of **Towns,** and the Nouns, **domus, rūs** and **humus.**

> e.g. $\left.\begin{array}{l}\textbf{Ad} \\ \textbf{In}\end{array}\right\}$ castra cucurrit. *He ran* $\left\{\begin{array}{l}\textit{to} \\ \textit{into}\end{array}\right\}$ *the camp.*

> $\left.\begin{array}{l}\overline{\textbf{E}} \\ \overline{\textbf{A}}\end{array}\right\}$ castrīs fūgit. *He fled* $\left\{\begin{array}{l}\textit{out of} \\ \textit{from}\end{array}\right\}$ *the camp.*
> **In** castrīs manēbat. *He remained in the camp.*

But Rōmam īvit. *He went to Rome.*
    Londīniō vēnit. *He came from London.*

N.B. (i) The following table

	TO	FROM	AT/IN/ON
home	domum	domō	domī
country	rūs	rūre	rūrī
ground	ad, in humum	humō	humī

(ii) Prepositions must be used with the names of **Countries.**

> e.g. **Ad** Britanniam. *To Britain.*
> **Ex** Hispaniā. *From Spain.*

(b) To translate **in** or **at** with the name of a town, the **Genitive Singular** is used if the name of the town is **Singular** and belongs to the **First** or **Second Declension.** Otherwise the **Dative Case** is used. This is known as the **Locative Case.**

	TO	FROM	IN/AT
Rome	Rōmam	Rōmā	Rōmae
Athens	Athēnās	Athēnīs	Athēnīs
London	Londīnium	Londīniō	Londīniī
Carthage	Carthāginem	Carthāgine	Carthāginī
Naples	Neāpolim	Neāpolī	Neāpolī
Cadiz	Gadēs	Gadibus	Gadibus

99. *Space*

All **Measurement** goes into the **Accusative Case. No Preposition.**

> e.g. **Decem mīlia passuum** prōgressī sumus.
> *We advanced ten miles.*
> Flūmen **centum pedēs** lātum.
> *A river one hundred feet broad.*

XIX. SIMPLE CONSTRUCTIONS

100. *Direct Question*

(*a*) In Latin a **Direct Question** can be expressed by
  (i) an **Interrogative** word.
  (ii) -ne, when no definite answer is expected.
  (iii) Nōnne, when the answer **Yes** is expected.
  (iv) Num, when the answer **No** is expected.

e.g. **Quis** es? **Quid** fēcistī? **Quandō** discēdēs?
  Who are you? What have you done? When will you leave?
  Potes**ne** hōc intellegere?
  Can you understand this?
  Nōnne hōc intellegis?
  ⎰Surely *you understand this?*
  ⎱*You understand this,* don't *you?*
  ⎱Don't *you understand this?*
  Num hōc intellegis?
  ⎰Surely *you do* not *understand this?*
  ⎱*You* don't *understand this,* do you?

N.B. –**ne** is added to the **first** word, but not to a preposition.

(*b*) In Latin a **Double Direct Question** can be expressed by
  (i) **Utrum . . . an (annōn)**
  (ii) **-ne . . . an (annōn)**
  (iii) **— . . . an (annōn)**

  ⎧**Utrum** Londīniī **an** Lutētiae manēbis?
e.g. ⎨Londīnii**ne** manēbis **an** Lutētiae?
  ⎩Londīniī **an** Lutētiae manēbis?
  (*Whether*) *will you remain in London or Paris?*
  ⎰**Utrum** vīnum amās **annōn?**
  ⎱Vīnum**ne** amās **annōn?**
  Do you like wine or not?

101. *Direct Commands and Prohibitions*

Latin expresses a Direct Command in the Second Person by using the **Imperative**. A Command in the First or Third Person is expressed by the **Present Subjunctive**. A Prohibition in the Second Person is expressed by **nōlī(te)** with the **Present Infinitive.** A Prohibition in the First or Third Person is expressed by **nē** with the **Present Subjunctive.** Thus in table form

	+ VE	− VE
First Person	**Present Subjunctive**	**Nē + Present Subjunctive**
Second Person	**Present Imperative**	**Nōlī(te) + Present Infinitive**
Third Person	**Present Subjunctive**	**Nē + Present Subjunctive**

> e.g. **Veniāmus.** *Let us come.*
> **Manē.** *Stay.*
> **Redeant.** *Let them return.*
> **Nē redeāmus.** *Let us not return.*
> **Nōlī manēre.** *Don't stay.*

N.B. Nē + Perfect Subjunctive may be used instead of **nōlī.**

> e.g. **Nē secūtus sīs.** *Don't follow.*

102. *Wishes*

In Latin the **Subjunctive** is used to express a **Wish** with **utinam,** negative **utinam nē.**

(*a*) A **Wish** for the **Future** is expressed by **utinam + Present Subjunctive.**

> e.g. **Utinam** falsus vātēs **sim.** *O that I may be a false prophet.*

(*b*) A **Wish** for the **Present** is expressed by **utinam + Imperfect Subjunctive.**

> e.g. **Utinam nē adessēs.** *Would that you were not here.*

(*c*) A **Wish** for the **Past** is expressed by **utinam + Pluperfect Subjunctive.**

> e.g. **Utinam** Rōmae **mānsissēs.**
> $\begin{Bmatrix} Would\ that \\ If\ only \end{Bmatrix}$ *you had stayed in Rome.*

XX. SUBORDINATE CONSTRUCTIONS

103. *Ablative Absolute*

(*a*) In Latin a **Noun** or **Pronoun** in the **Ablative Case** is often used with a **Participle** in agreement to express the idea of **Time, Cause,** and **Concession.** This is known as an **Ablative Absolute.** The **Noun** or **Pronoun** and **Participle** have no **grammatical** connection with the rest of the sentence.

> e.g. **Urbe incēnsā,** Rōmānī sē recēpērunt.
>
> *When*
> *After* ⎫
> *Since* ⎬ *the city had been burned, the Romans retreated.*
> *Although* ⎭

(*b*) The **Perfect Participle** is the Participle most commonly found in this construction, but the **Present Participle** is used very often to express the idea of **Time.** The Future Participle rarely occurs in an Ablative Absolute.

> e.g. **Mē redeunte,** turris incēnsa est.
> *While I was returning, the tower was burned.*

N.B. An Ablative Absolute can only be used if the **Participle** agrees with neither the **Subject** nor the **Object** of the **Main Verb.**

(*c*) As the Verb **to be** does not have a Present Participle, it is possible to have an Ablative Absolute consisting of **Two Nouns** or a **Noun** and an **Adjective** with the Participle 'being' understood.

> e.g. **Numā rēge,** lit. *Numa being king, in the reign of Numa.*
> Thus
> > **Caesare duce,** *under the leadership of Caesar*
> > **meā mātre vīvā,** *in my mother's lifetime*
> > **mē īnsciō,** *without my knowledge*
> > **tē auctōre,** *at your instigation*
> > **adversō flūmine,** *upstream*
> > **secundō flūmine,** *downstream*
> > **nōbīs invītīs,** *against our will*
> > **Cicerōne cōnsule,** *in the consulship of Cicero*

104. *Indirect Statement*

(*a*) Veniam. *I shall come,* is a Direct Statement. Dīxī **mē ventūrum esse.** *I said that I would come,* is an **Indirect**

Statement. Thus an **Indirect Statement** is a **Noun Clause** objective after Verbs of **saying, thinking, believing, etc.** In Latin the **Subject** of the **Noun Clause** goes into the **Accusative,** the **Verb** of the **Noun Clause** goes into the **Infinitive.**

> e.g. Sciēbāmus **urbem captam esse.**
> *We knew the city had been captured.*

The following table shows how to translate the **Infinitive.**

> Present Infinitive = *is, was, were.*
> Perfect Infinitive = *have, has, had.*
> Future Infinitive = *will, would.*

e.g. Putāmus puellam $\begin{cases} \textbf{venīre.} \\ \textbf{vēnisse.} \\ \textbf{ventūram esse.} \end{cases}$

We think (that) the girl $\begin{cases} \textit{is coming.} \\ \textit{has come.} \\ \textit{will come.} \end{cases}$

Putābāmus puellam $\begin{cases} \textbf{venīre.} \\ \textbf{vēnisse.} \\ \textbf{ventūram esse.} \end{cases}$

We thought (that) the girl $\begin{cases} \textit{was coming.} \\ \textit{had come.} \\ \textit{would come.} \end{cases}$

N.B. When translating into Latin beware of **was, were** after a **Present Tense** when a **Perfect Infinitive** is required.

> e.g. Scīmus puellam **fuisse** fēlīcem.
> *We know (that) the girl was happy.*

(*b*) **Sē** is used if (i) the **Subject** of the **Infinitive** is the **same** as that of the **Main Verb** and is **Third Person,** (ii) the **Object** of the **Infinitive** is the **same** as the **Subject** of the **Main Verb** and is **Third Person.**

> e.g. Dīxit **sē** ventūrum esse. He *said he would come.*
> Dīxit nōs **sibi** persuāsisse. He *said we had persuaded* him.

Eum, eam, etc. are used when the **Subject** or **Object** is different.

e.g. Dīximus $\begin{cases} \textbf{eam} \text{ interfectam esse.} \\ \textbf{eam eōs} \text{ interfectūram esse.} \end{cases}$

We said that $\begin{cases} \textit{she had been killed.} \\ \textit{she would kill them.} \end{cases}$

(*c*) **Spērō,** *I hope,* **promittō,** *I promise,* **iūrō,** *I swear,* **minor,** *I threaten* are followed by an **Accusative** and **Future Infinitive.**

e.g. Spērābant **sē ventūrōs esse.** *They hoped to come.*
Prōmīsimus **nōs mānsūrōs esse.** *We promised to stay.*

(*d*) **Negō,** *I deny, say* . . . *not,* is used; never dico . . . non.

e.g. **Negāvit** sē ventūrum esse. *He said he would not come.*

Thus, **negāre quemquam,** *to say that* . . . *no one*
negāre quidquam, *to say that* . . . *nothing*
negāre umquam, *to say that* . . . *never*
negāre usquam, *to say that* . . . *nowhere*

105. *Rule of Sequence*

In many Latin constructions in which the **Subjunctive** is used, the **Rule of Sequence** is observed. This is a simple method of dividing English tenses into two groups. This rule applies to the **Main Verb** and the **Tense** of the **Subjunctive** to be used will depend on the **Sequence** of the **Main Verb.**

Present
Future
Perfect with have } **Primary Tenses of the Indicative.**
Imperative
Future Perfect

Imperfect
Perfect without have } **Historic (Secondary) Tenses of the Indicative.**
Pluperfect

106. *Indirect Command*

(*a*) Venī, *Come,* is a Direct Command
Mē rogāvit **ut venīrem,** *He asked me to come,* is an **Indirect**

Command. Thus in Latin **ut** is used, negative **nē** with a **Present** or **Imperfect Subjunctive** according to **Sequence** to express an **Indirect Command.** This construction occurs after such verbs as **moneō,** *I warn,* **rogō,** *I ask,* **imperō,** *I order,* etc.

e.g. Mihi imperāvit **ut festīnārem.** *He ordered me to hurry.*
Monēbuntur **nē canant.** *They will be advised not to sing.*

N.B. In English an **Indirect Command** is most often shown by a **plain Infinitive.**

(*b*) Only two Latin Verbs take the English construction, **iubeō,** *I order,* and **vetō,** *I order . . . not, forbid.*

e.g. Iussī eōs **sequī.** *I* $\begin{Bmatrix} ordered \\ told \end{Bmatrix}$ *them to follow.*

Vetuī eōs **sequī.** *I* $\begin{Bmatrix} ordered \\ told \end{Bmatrix}$ *them not to follow.*

N.B. Iubeō and **vetō** may be translated by **tell** in the sense of **order.**

(*c*) **Sē** is used if the **Object** of the **Subordinate Verb** is the same as the **Subject** of the **Main Verb** and is **Third Person.**

e.g. Nōs hortātus est ut **sibi** librum ostenderēmus.
He urged us to show him *the book.*

107. *Indirect Question*

(*a*) Quid dīcis? *What are you saying?* is a Direct Question. Nesciō **quid dīcās?** *I do not know what you are saying,* is an **Indirect Question.** Thus in Latin the **Verb** of the **Indirect Question** goes into the **Subjunctive** and the clause is introduced by such words as **quis, quid, quandō, quārē, quot** etc. **Six Subjunctives** may be used.

Main Verb Primary $\begin{cases} \textbf{Present Subjunctive} \\ \textbf{Perfect Subjunctive} \\ \textbf{-ūrus sim} \ (will) \end{cases}$

Main Verb Historic $\begin{cases} \textbf{Imperfect Subjunctive} \\ \textbf{Pluperfect Subjunctive} \\ \textbf{-ūrus essem} \ (would) \end{cases}$

Golden Rule
The Verb in the **Principal Clause** decides the **Sequence,**
the verb in the **Subordinate Clause** decides the **Tense** of
the **Subjunctive** to be used.

e.g. Nesciō **quandō** $\begin{cases} \textbf{redeās.} \\ \textbf{redieris.} \\ \textbf{reditūrus sīs.} \end{cases}$

I do not know when you $\begin{cases} \textit{are returning.} \\ \textit{returned.} \\ \textit{will return.} \end{cases}$

Nesciēbam **quid** $\begin{cases} \textbf{facerēs.} \\ \textbf{fēcissēs.} \\ \textbf{factūrus essēs.} \end{cases}$

I did not know what you $\begin{cases} \textit{were doing.} \\ \textit{had done.} \\ \textit{would do.} \end{cases}$

(*b*) **Num,** *if*, *whether*

Utrum . . . an(necne), $\begin{cases} \textit{if . . .} \\ \textit{whether} \end{cases}$ *or* (*not*) are also used to
introduce **Indirect Questions.**

e.g. Certior nōn factus est **utrum** pervēnissēs **necne.**

He was not told $\begin{cases} \textit{if} \\ \textit{whether} \end{cases}$ *you had arrived or not.*

(*c*) **Sē** is used as in Indirect Command to refer to the **Subject**
of the **Main Verb.**

e.g. Rogāvit num **sē** adiūtūrī essēmus.
He asked if we would help him.

108. *Purpose Clauses*
(*a*) In Latin **ut,** negative **nē,** is used with the **Present** or
Imperfect Subjunctive according to **Sequence** to express
the **Purpose** of an action.

e.g. Venit **ut** rēgīnam **videat**.

He is coming $\begin{cases} in\ order\ that\ he\ may\ see\ the\ queen. \\ in\ order\ to\ see\ the\ queen. \\ to\ see\ the\ queen. \end{cases}$

Domī manēbant **nē vidērentur**.

They stayed at home $\begin{cases} in\ order\ that\ they\ might\ not\ be\ seen. \\ in\ order\ not\ to\ be\ seen. \end{cases}$

(*b*) **Quō** is used instead of **ut** if the **Purpose Clause** contains a **Comparative Adjective** or **Adverb**.

e.g. Collem ascendērunt **quō facilius** vallem vidērent.
They climbed the hill to see the valley more easily.

(*c*) **Quī – quae – quod** is often used instead of **ut** when there is an **Antecedent** in the **Accusative Case.**

e.g. **Gladium** mihi dedit **quō** ūterer.
He gave me a sword to use.
Lintrem inveniam in **quā** flūmen trānseam.
I shall find a boat in which to cross the river.

(*d*) **Sē** is used to refer to the **Subject** of the **Main Verb** if **Third Person.**

e.g. Hanc ōrātiōnem habuit nē **sē** culpārēmus.
He made this speech that we might not blame him.

For other ways of expressing Purpose, vid. secs. 95, 96, 128.

109. *Result Clauses*
(*a*) In Latin **ut,** negative **ut nōn,** with the **Subjunctive** is used to express the **Result** of an action.

e.g. Tam sapienter dīcit **ut** omnibus **persuādeat**.
He speaks so wisely that he persuades everybody.
Tantum saxum erat **ut nēmō** id tollere **posset**.
The stone was so big that no one could lift it.
Hostēs tot erant **ut fūgerimus**.
The enemy were so numerous that we fled.

N.B. In a Result Clause the **Perfect Subjunctive** may be used to stress the fact that the result actually did occur, i.e. **a once and for all action.**

(*b*) **Tam,** *so,* is used with **Adjectives** or **Adverbs.**
Ita, adeō, *so,* are used with **Verbs.**

> e.g. **Adeō** īrāscēbātur ut omnēs eum timerēmus.
> *He was so angry that we all feared him.*

N.B. Sē is **not** used to refer to Subject of Main Verb if Third Person.

(*c*) Note the following table.

	PURPOSE	RESULT
so that not	**nē**	**ut nōn**
so that no one	**nē quis**	**ut nēmō**
so that nothing	**nē quid**	**ut nihil**
so that none	**nē** $\begin{cases} \text{ūllus} \\ \text{quī} \end{cases}$	**ut nūllus**
so that never	**nē umquam**	**ut numquam**
so that nowhere	**nē usquam**	**ut nusquam**

110. *Conditional Clauses*

(*a*) In Latin the **Indicative** is used in the **if** clause when the **Principal Clause** makes a **plain statement of fact.**

> e.g. Sī hōc **facis,** stultus es.
> *If you do this, you are foolish.*
> Sī hōc **fēcistī,** stultus erās.
> *If you did this, you were foolish.*
> Sī hōc **fēceris,** poenās dabis.
> *If you do this, you will be punished.*

N.B. (i) Latin logically uses the **Future Perfect** in the last example as it argues that you cannot be punished until **you will have done this.**

(**ii**) Latin uses the **Future** when the **if** verb is going on at the **same time** as the **Main Verb.**

> e.g. Sī Rōmae **eris,** tē vīsam.
> *If you are in Rome, I shall visit you.*

These are often called **Open Conditions.**

(*b*) In Latin the **Subjunctive** is used in **both** clauses when the **Principal Clause** merely states a **possibility,** i.e. that something **would, should** or **would have** happened.

> e.g. Sī hōc **faciās,** poenās **dēs.**
>> *If you were to do this, you would be punished.*
>> Sī hōc **facerēs,** fēlīx **essēs.**
>> *If you were doing this, you would be happy.*
>> Sī hōc **fēcissēs,** poenās **dedissēs.**
>> *If you had done this, you would have been punished.*
>
> Thus in table form

2 × Present Subjunctive = *were to* . . . $\begin{cases} would \\ should \end{cases}$

2 × Imperfect Subjunctive = *were* . . . $\begin{cases} would \\ should \end{cases}$

2 × Pluperfect Subjunctive = *had* . . . $\begin{cases} would \\ should \end{cases}$ *have*

Such Conditions referring to the **Present** or **Past** are often called **Unfulfilled Conditions.**

(*c*) **Sī** = *if*
 Nisi = *unless*

Sī . . . non = *if . . . not* (where only **one** word is negatived not the whole clause).

> e.g. Sī librum, **nōn** tabulam ēmerit, gaudēbō.
>> *If he buys a book not a picture, I shall be glad.*
> **Si quis** = *if anyone.*

111. *Verbs of Fearing*

In Latin Verbs of Fearing, e.g. **timeō, vereor** are followed by **nē** if **Positive, nē nōn** or **ut** if **Negative** with the **Present** or **Perfect Subjunctive** after a **Primary Main Verb,** the **Imperfect** or **Pluperfect** after an **Historic Main Verb.**

> e.g. Timeō **nē redeat.**
>> *I am afraid that he* $\begin{cases} is\ returning. \\ may\ return. \\ will\ return. \end{cases}$

Verēbar **ut redīret.**

I feared that he $\begin{cases} \textit{was not returning.} \\ \textit{might not return.} \\ \textit{would not return.} \end{cases}$

Timēmus **nē nōn redierit.**
We fear that he has not returned.

N.B. (i) Ut can be used for **nē nōn** after **vereor** if positive, **timeō** always takes **nē nōn.**

(ii) Verbs of Fearing can be followed by an **Infinitive.**

e.g. Timēbat **loquī.**
He was afraid to speak.

(iii) Sē is used to refer to **Subject** of **Main Verb** if **Third Person.**

e.g. Mīles vulnerātus verēbātur ut **sē** vīdissēmus.
The wounded soldier feared we had not seen him.

112. *Verbs of Doubting*

Dubitō, *I doubt* and **dubius,** *doubtful* if **Negative** are followed by **quīn** with **Six Subjunctives.**

e.g. Nōn dubitāmus **quīn** novae cōpiae $\begin{cases} \textbf{perveniant.} \\ \textbf{pervēnerint.} \\ \textbf{perventūrae sint.} \end{cases}$

We $\begin{cases} \textit{do not doubt} \\ \textit{have no doubt} \end{cases}$ *that reinforcements* $\begin{cases} \textit{are arriving.} \\ \textit{have arrived.} \\ \textit{will arrive.} \end{cases}$

Haud dubium erat **quīn** nāvis $\begin{cases} \textbf{venīret.} \\ \textbf{vēnisset.} \\ \textbf{ventūra esset.} \end{cases}$

There was no doubt that the ship $\begin{cases} \textit{was coming.} \\ \textit{had come.} \\ \textit{would come.} \end{cases}$

N.B. (i) $\begin{matrix} \textbf{Quis} \\ \textbf{Vix quisquam} \end{matrix}$ dubitat, $\begin{cases} \textit{Who} \\ \textit{scarcely anyone} \end{cases}$ doubts, count as **Negative** and are therefore followed by **quīn** with the **Subjunctive.**

(ii) Sē is used to refer to **Subject** of **Main Verb** if **Third Person.**

> e.g. Captīvus nōn dubitābat quīn **sē** ēreptūrī essēmus.
> *The* captive *had no doubt that we would save* him.

(iii) Dubitō if **Negative** and followed by an **Infinitive** means *I hesitate.*

> e.g. Puer **nōn** dubitāvit pilam **iacere.**
> *The boy did not hesitate to throw the ball.*

113. *Simple Causal Clauses*

(*a*) **Quod, quia,** *because,* **quoniam,** *since, as,* are followed by the **Indicative.**

> e.g. Puella lacrimābat $\begin{Bmatrix} \textbf{quod} \\ \textbf{quia} \end{Bmatrix}$ canem **amīserat.**
> *The girl was crying because she had lost her dog.*
> **Quoniam vēnistī, mē** adiuvāre dēbēs.
> *Since you have come, you ought to help me.*

(*b*) **Cum,** *since, as,* is followed by the **Subjunctive.**

> e.g. **Cum** ad flūmen **advēnisset,** pontem trānsīre cōnstituit.
> *Since he had reached the river, he decided to cross the bridge.*

114. *Simple Concessive Clauses*

(*a*) **Quamquam,** *although,* is followed by the **Indicative.**

> e.g. **Quamquam** hostēs superiōrēs numerō **erant,** eōs adortī sumus.
> *Although the enemy were superior in numbers, we attacked them.*

(*b*) **Cum,** *although,* is followed by the **Subjunctive.**

> e.g. **Cum** īnferiōrēs numerō **essēmus,** in hostēs impetum fēcimus.
> *Although we were inferior in numbers, we attacked the enemy.*

115. *Temporal Clauses*

Dum

(*a*) **Dum,** *while, as long as,* is always followed by the **Indicative.** A **Present Indicative** is used if the **dum** Verb lasts **longer** than the Main Verb. If the **dum Verb,** lasts the **same** length of time as the **Main Verb,** it goes into the **same** tense as the **Main Verb.**

> e.g. **Dum** Rōmae **sum,** Cicerōnem vīdī.
> *While I was in Rome, I saw Cicero.*
> **Dum** Rōmae **eram,** apud Cicerōnem **manēbam.**
> *While I was in Rome, I stayed with Cicero.*
> **Dum** Rōmae **eris,** apud Cicerōnem **manēbis.**
> *As long as you are in Rome, you will stay with Cicero.*

(*b*) **Dum,** *until,* takes the **Indicative** if nothing but **Pure Time** is indicated, i.e. that the action simply took place.

> e.g. **Dum** nūntius **rediit,** pavor in urbe erat.
> *Until the messenger returned, there was panic in the city.*

Dōnec, quoad, *until,* are often found in this type of clause.

(*c*) **Dum,** *until,* takes the **Subjunctive, Present** or **Imperfect** when **Purpose** or **Design** is implied, frequently after **Verbs** of **waiting.**

> e.g. **Sedē** ibī **dum redeam.**
> *Sit there until I return.*
> **Exspectābant dum** novae cōpiae in cōnspectum **venīrent.**
> *They waited* { *until the reinforcements should come into view.*
> { *for the reinforcements to come into view.*

116. *Cum*

(*a*) **Cum,** *when,* takes the **Indicative** if the **Main Verb** is **Primary.**

> e.g. **Cum** tēcum **sum,** fēlīx sum.
> *When I am with you, I am happy.*
> **Cum** Rōmam **vēneris,** Cicerōnem vidēbis.
> *When you come (i.e. will have come) to Rome, you will see Cicero.*
> **Cum** Rōmae **eris,** lūdōs vidēbis.
> *When you are (i.e. will be) in Rome, you will see the games.*

Note the accuracy of the Latin tenses.

(*b*) **Cum,** *when,* takes the **Subjunctive (Imperfect** or **Pluperfect)** if the **Main Verb** is **Historic.**

e.g. **Cum** ad flūmen **vēnissent,** ad alteram rīpam nāvērunt.
    When they came to the river, they swam to the other bank.
    Cum per silvam **ambulāret,** lupum vīdit.
    When he was walking through the wood, he saw a wolf.

(*c*) **Cum,** *whenever,* takes the **Perfect Indicative** if the **Main Verb** is **Primary,** the **Pluperfect Indicative** if the **Main Verb** is **Historic.**

e.g. **Cum** mē **vīdit,** rīdet.
    Whenever he sees me, he smiles.
    Cum mē **vīderat,** rīdēbat.

    Whenever he saw me, he $\begin{cases} \textit{smiled.} \\ \textit{would smile.} \end{cases}$

117. *Ubī, Postquam, Simulac*

(*a*) **Ubī,** *when,* **postquam,** *after,* **simulac,** *as soon as,* take a **Perfect Indicative** if the **Main Verb** is **Historic.**

    $\left.\begin{array}{l} \textbf{Ubī} \\ \text{e.g. } \textbf{Postquam} \\ \textbf{Simulac} \end{array}\right\}$ **cōnfessus est,** capitis damnātus est.

    $\left.\begin{array}{l} \textit{When} \\ \textit{After} \\ \textit{As soon as} \end{array}\right\}$ *he (had) confessed, he was condemned to death.*

(*b*) Only **postquam** can take a **Pluperfect Indicative** if a **definite** period of time is mentioned.

e.g. **Decem post diēbus quam redierat,** mortem obiit.
    Ten days after he had returned, he died.

N.B. Ubī, simulac may be followed by a **Future** a **Future Perfect** like **cum.**

    e.g. $\left.\begin{array}{l} \textbf{Ubī} \\ \textbf{Simulac} \end{array}\right\}$ **pervēneris,** rēgem vidēbis.

    $\left.\begin{array}{l} \textit{When} \\ \textit{As soon as} \end{array}\right\}$ *you arrive, you will see the king.*

118. *Antequam, Priusquam*

(*a*) **Antequam, priusquam,** *before,* take the **Indicative** if nothing but **Pure Time** is indicated, i.e. that the action simply took place.

e.g. Mīlitem **prius** interfēcit **quam pervēnī.**
He killed the soldier before I arrived.
Antequam cubitum **eō,** fenestram aperiam.
Before I go to bed, I shall open the window.
Nōn **prius** discēdam **quam** mihi vēra **dīxeris.**

I shall not leave $\begin{Bmatrix} before \\ until \end{Bmatrix}$ *you tell me the truth.*

N.B. Latin tenses used with **priusquam** and **antequam** are the **same** as those used in English except if the **Main Verb** is **Negative Future** when a **Future Perfect** is used in the 'before' clause.

(*b*) **Antequam, priusquam** take a **Present** or **Imperfect Subjunctive** when **Purpose** or **Design** is implied, i.e. that the action of the Main Verb takes place before that of the Subordinate Verb **can** happen.

e.g. **Priusquam** portās **clauderent,** armātī in oppidum ruērunt.
Before they could close the gates, armed men rushed into the town.
Puer ex agrō **prius** cucurrit **quam** agricola **sē prohibēret.**
The boy ran from the field before the farmer could stop him.

N.B. **Sē** is used to refer to the **Subject** of the **Main Verb** as **Purpose** is implied.

119. *Comparative Clauses*
(*a*) In Latin the **Indicative** is used to indicate a **Real Comparison,** i.e. English **'as'.**

e.g. Mea māter **eadem** est $\begin{Bmatrix} \textbf{ac} \\ \textbf{quae} \end{Bmatrix}$ abhinc annōs vīgintī **erat.**

My mother is the same as she was twenty years ago.
Tot aquilās nōn vīdimus **quot exspectābāmus.**
We did not see as many eagles as we expected.
Tam fortis est **quam** leō.
He is as brave as a lion.

The following list contains the common phrases used in Latin to introduce a **Real Comparison.**

tam . . . quam	*as . . . as*
tantus . . . quantus	*as great . . . as*
tot . . . quot	*as many . . . as*
tālis . . . quālis	*such a kind . . . as*
totiēs . . . quotiēs	*so often . . . as*
īdem . . . $\left\{\begin{array}{l}\text{ac}\\\text{quī}\end{array}\right\}$	*the same . . . as*
sīcut	*just as*
haud $\left\{\begin{array}{l}\text{aliter}\\\text{secus}\end{array}\right\}$ ac	*not otherwise than*
perinde ac	*exactly as*

(*b*) In Latin the **Subjunctive** is used to indicate an **Imaginary Comparison,** i.e. English '**as if**'.

e.g. Sē gerit **velutsī** īnsānus **esset.**
He behaves as if he were mad.
Sē gessit **velutsī** imāginem **vīdisset.**
He behaved as if he had seen a ghost.

N.B. Velutsī observes **Conditional** rules, **quasi** observes **Sequence** rules.

e.g. Sē gerit **quasi** īnsānus **sit.**

120. *Sub-Oblique Clauses, i.e. Subordinate Clauses in Reported Speech.*
In Latin if an **Adjective** or **Adverbial Clause** is **Subordinate** to an **Indirect Statement, Command** or **Question,** i.e. is **part** of the **direct words** its **Verb** goes into the **Subjunctive.**

e.g. DIRECT
Cum mīles redierit, eum vidēbimus.
When the soldier returns, we shall see him.

INDIRECT
Dīximus nōs, cum mīles **rediisset,** eum vīsūrōs esse.
We said that when the soldier returned we would see him.

DIRECT
> Cur librum quem tibi dedī, amīsistī?
> *Why have you lost the book I gave you?*

INDIRECT
> Scīre volō cur librum quem tibi **dederim,** amīseris.
> *I want to know why you have lost the book I gave you.*

DIRECT
> Recitā carmen quod didicistī.
> *Recite the poem you have learned.*

INDIRECT
> Magister mē iussit carmen quod **didicissem** recitāre.
> *The teacher told me to recite the poem I had learned.*

N.B. The **Tense** of the Subjunctive to be used is found by going back to the **Direct Words** and then applying the following table.

DIRECT TENSE	MAIN VERB PRIMARY	MAIN VERB HISTORIC
Present	**Present Subjunctive**	**Imperfect Subjunctive**
Imperfect	**Imperfect Subjunctive**	**Imperfect Subjunctive**
Perfect	**Perfect Subjunctive**	**Pluperfect Subjunctive**
Pluperfect	**Pluperfect Subjunctive**	**Pluperfect Subjunctive**
Future	**Present Subjunctive**	**Imperfect Subjunctive**
Future Perfect	**Perfect Subjunctive**	**Pluperfect Subjunctive**

Additional Syntax

XXI. NOUNS

121. *Accusative*

(*a*) The **Accusative** is found, particularly in poetry, after an **Adjective** to define more exactly the meaning of the **Adjective**.

> e.g. Flāva **comās.** *Fair haired.* (lit. *fair as to the hair.*)
> Fēminae nūdae **bracchia** et **lacertōs.**
> *Women with their lower and upper arms bare.*
> (lit. *women bare as to their lower and upper arms.*)

(*b*) The **Accusative** is found, particularly in poetry, after a **Perfect Participle Passive** to denote the **part of the body** affected.

> e.g. **Femur** trāgulā ictus.
> *Wounded in the thigh by a javelin.*
> (lit. *wounded as to the thigh. . . .*)
> Subtūsa **genās.** *With her cheeks bruised.*
> (lit. *bruised as to her cheeks.*)

(*c*) The **Accusative** is found, mostly in poetry, after a **Passive Verb** which is really **Reflexive** in meaning, i.e. the **Subject** is doing something to or for **himself.**

> e.g. **Lōrīcam** induitur. *He dons his breastplate.*
> Laevō suspēnsī **loculōs tabulāsque** lacertō.
> *Slinging their schoolbags and writing pads over their left arms.*
> Conversī **lūmina.** *Turning their eyes.*

122. *Genitive*

(*a*) The **Genitive** may follow another Noun to denote that the **Genitive** is the **Subject** of the activity.

> e.g. Timor **populī**. *The fear of the people.* (i.e. *the people fear.*)
> Veterēs **Helvētiōrum** iniūriae.
> *The ancient wrongs of the Helvetii.*
> (i.e. *The Helvetii committed ancient wrongs.*)

(*b*) The **Genitive** may follow another Noun to denote that the **Genitive** is the **Object** of the activity.

> e.g. Timor **populī**. *The fear of the people.* (i.e. *we fear the people.*)
> Veterēs Helvētiōrum iniūriae **populī Rōmānī**.
> *The ancient wrongs of the Helvetii on the Roman people.*
> (i.e. *The Helvetii wronged the Roman people.*)

(*c*) The **Genitive** is used with the verb **to be** to mean, *duty of, mark of, characteristic of.*

> e.g. **Mīlitis** est pugnāre. *It is the duty of a soldier to fight.*
> **Discipulōrum** est tempus terere.
> *It is characteristic of pupils to waste time.*

123. *Dative*

(*a*) The **Dative** is sometimes used after a **Perfect Passive** to denote the **Agent**.

> e.g. Rēs tōta **mihi** prōvīsa est.
> *The whole business has been arranged by me.*

(For Dative of Agent after Gerundive, vid. sec. 96b.)

(*b*) The **Dative** is used to indicate the **purpose aimed at** (vid. sec. 73c).

> e.g. **Receptuī** cecinit. *He sounded the retreat.*
> Comitia **cēnsōribus creāndīs** habuit.
> *He held a meeting for electing censors.*

(*c*) The **Dative** is used in poetry to indicate **motion towards**.

> e.g. It clamor **caelō**. *The shouting reaches the heavens.*

(*d*) The **Dative** of a **Pronoun** can be used to indicate a person **interested** in the action.

> e.g. Quid **mihi** Celsus agit? *How, please, is Celsus doing?*

124. *Ablative*

(*a*) The **Ablative** is used with a **Comparative** to indicate how much something or somebody is **different** from something or somebody else.

> e.g. Hibernia **dīmidiō** minor est quam Britannia.
> *Ireland is half as small as Britain.*
> **Paulō** ⎫   ⎧*little*   ⎫
> **Aliquantō** ⎬ altior est. *He is* ⎨*considerably* ⎬ *taller.*
> **Multō** ⎭   ⎩*much*   ⎭

(*b*) The **Ablative** is used to indicate **Separation.**

> e.g. **Dēfēnsōribus** castra nūdāvit.
> *He stripped the camp of defenders.*
> Hostēs **commeātū** intercludere cōnstituit.
> *He decided to cut the enemy off from their supplies.*

(*c*) The **Ablative** is used to define more closely in what **Respect** the statement is made.

> e.g. Quattuor mīlia **numerō.** *Four thousand in number.*
> Ferōx **ingeniō.** *Fierce in character.*
> Captus **alterō oculō.** *Blind in one eye.*

XXII. RELATIVE CLAUSES

125. (*a*) A **Superlative** or **Numeral Adjective** is attracted from the **Antecedent** into the **Relative Clause.**

> e.g. Equōs quōs **optimōs** habeō, vendam.
> *I shall sell the best horses I have.*
> Barbarō quem **prīmum** vīdit pepercit.
> *He spared the first native he saw.*

(*b*) The **Antecedent** is often repeated in the **Relative Clause.**

> e.g. Silvam prope castra sitam animadvertit quā in **silvā** equitēs
> cēlāvit.
> *He spotted a wood near the camp in which he hid his cavalry.*

XXIII. VERBS

126. *Epistolary Imperfect*

The **Imperfect** is often used in **letters** to refer to the time of writing, i.e. the writer puts himself in the place of the recipient and uses the **Imperfect** for the Present.

> e.g. Nihil **habēbam** quod plūs scrīberem.
> *I have nothing more to write.*

127. *Indicative*

The following idiomatic use of the **Indicative** should be noted.

> Facile **est**. *It would be easy.*
>
> Facile $\left\{ \begin{matrix} \textbf{erat} \\ \textbf{fuit} \end{matrix} \right\}$. *It would have been easy.*

128. *First Supine*

The **First Supine** is used after **Verbs of Motion** to express **Purpose.**

> e.g. **Cubitum** īvērunt. *They went to bed.*
> Tertiam cohortem **frūmentātum** mīsit.
> *He sent the third cohort to forage.*

129. *Subjunctive*

(*a*) In Latin the **Subjunctive** is used when a **Question** is asked implying **bewilderment** or **indecision**. This is called a **Deliberative Question.**

> e.g. Quid **dīcam**? *What am I to say?*
> Quid **dīcerem**? *What was I to say?*
> Quō **īrent**? *Where were they to go?*

(*b*) In Latin the **Subjunctive** is used to express a **Possibility,** really a **Condition** with the **if** clause omitted. This is called a **Potential Subjunctive.**

> **Velim** venīre.   *I should like to come.*
> **Vellem** venīre.   *I should have liked to come.*
> **Velim** veniās.   *I should like you to come.*
> **Vellem** vēnissēs.   *I should have liked you to come.*

N.B. The subjunctives **veniās** and **vēnisses** are best taken as Wishes for the Future and Past respectively, i.e. *I should like you to come* = *O that you may come.*

XXIV. PLACE

130. (*a*) In Latin it is possible to have a **Double Accusative** of **Motion.**

> e.g. **In castra ad ducem** vēnit.
> *He came to the general in the camp.*

(*b*) In Latin **ad** is found with the **Name** of a **Town** to mean, *in the neighbourhood of,* or *in the direction of.*

> e.g. Proelium **ad Cannās** factum.
> *The battle fought at Cannae.*
> **Ad Ilerdam** proficīscitur.
> *He set out in the direction of Ilerda.*

(*c*) The Verb **absum** takes **a(b)** even with the **Names** of **Towns** as no motion is implied.

> e.g. Decem mīlia passuum **ā Vēiīs** aberant.
> *They were ten miles distant from Veii.*

(*d*) **Domus** may take the Preposition **in** when it means *house.*

> e.g. **In** domum iniit. *He entered the house.*

XXV. SUBORDINATE CONSTRUCTIONS

131. *Indirect Statement*

(*a*) As some Latin Verbs do not have a **Supine,** and therefore cannot form the **Future Infinitive, fore ut** with a **Present** or **Imperfect Subjunctive** is used as follows.

> e.g. Puer dīxit **fore ut** hōs versūs **disceret.**
> *The boy said he would learn these verses.*
> Prō certō habēmus **fore ut** nostrī hostibus **resistant.**
> *We are sure our men will resist the enemy.*

(*b*) In Indirect Statement the **Future Infinitive Passive** is somewhat rare, **fore ut** is usually preferred.

> e.g. Rēx certior factus est **fore ut** fēminae **servārentur.**
> *The king was informed that the women would be saved.*

(*c*) **Simulō,** *pretend* and **dissimulō,** *pretend . . . not,* are followed by an **Accusative** and **Infinitive.**

> e.g. Simulābāmus **nōs aegrōs esse.**
> *We pretended to be ill.*
> Puer dissimulābat **sē** librum **amīsisse.**
> *The boy pretended he had not lost the book.*

(*d*) **Vidētur,** *it seems,* **dīcitur,** *it is said,* **putātur,** *it is thought,* **nūntiātur,** *it is announced,* are used **Personally** in the **Present, Future** and **Imperfect Tenses.**

> e.g.**Vidēris** esse dīves.
> *It seems that you are rich.*
> **Putābāmur** interfectī esse.
> *It was thought that we had been killed.*

N.B. In the **Perfect Tenses** these Verbs are used **Impersonally** as in English.

> e.g. **Nūntiātum est** hostēs appropinquāre.
> *It was announced that the enemy were approaching.*

(*e*) Verbs of **Emotion,** e.g. **gaudeō,** *be glad,* **doleō,** *be sorry,* **mīror,** *be surprised that,* can be followed by (i) **Indirect Statement** (ii) **Quod** with the **Indicative.**

> e.g. Dolēbant $\begin{cases} \textbf{tē} \text{ nōn } \textbf{rediisse.} \\ \textbf{quod} \text{ nōn } \textbf{redierās.} \end{cases}$
> *They were sorry you had not returned.*

132. *Nēve, Neu*

If a **Positive Purpose Clause** or **Indirect Command** is followed by a **Negative One, nēve (neu)** introduces the **second** one.

> e.g. Rōmam vēnit ut studeat **nēve** tempus terat.
> *He has come to Rome to study and not to waste time.*
> Cōnsul suōs hortātus est ut resisterent **neu** sē traderent.
> *The consul encouraged his men to resist and not to surrender.*

133. *Quī Generic*

In Latin **quī** – **quae** – **quod** is often used with the **Subjunctive** to mean, *the sort of person to* or *the kind of person to.*

e.g. Is est **quī** urbem **servet.**

He is the man to save the city.

(lit. *he is the sort of person who may save the city.*)

Erant **quī** cōnsulem **culpārent.**

There were some who blamed the consul.

(lit. *there were those of the kind who might blame the consul.*)

Other such phrases are:

dīgnus est quī	*he deserves to*
ea est quae	*she is the woman to*
aptus est quī	*he is fit to*
nihil habeō quod	*I have nothing to*

134. *Comparison*

(*a*) In Latin the **Comparative** is used with **quam quī (ut)** and the **Subjunctive** to mean *too . . . to.*

e.g. Puer erat **stultior quam** $\begin{Bmatrix} \textbf{quī} \\ \textbf{ut} \end{Bmatrix}$ hunc librum **intellegeret.**

The boy was too stupid to understand this book.

Gladius est **gravior quam** $\begin{Bmatrix} \textbf{quem} \\ \textbf{ut} \end{Bmatrix}$ **tollam.**

The sword is too heavy for me to raise.

(*b*) In Latin **quō** and the **Comparative** followed by **eō** and the **Comparative** means *the more . . . the more.*

e.g. **Quō citius, eō melius.** *The sooner, the better.*

Quō plūs vīnī **quis** bibit, **eō magis** id amat.

The more wine a man drinks, the more he likes it.

N.B. Quis after **quō** means *a man* or *anyone.*

135. *Conditional Clauses*

(*a*) In Latin **sīve(seu) . . . sīve(seu)** introduce a **Double Condition.**

e.g. **Sīve** ille damnātus esset **sīve** absolūtus esset, nēmō eī
crēdidisset.

*Whether that man had been condemned or acquitted no one
would have believed him.*

Sīve Pompēiīs mānseris, **sīve nōn** mānseris, Rōmam redībimus.

Whether you stay in Pompeii or not, we shall return to Rome.

(*b*) In an **Unfulfilled Condition** it is possible to have the **sī** clause referring to **Past Time** and the **Principal Clause** to **Present Time.**

e.g. Sī dīligentius **labōrāvissēmus,** hodiē dīvitēs **essēmus.**
If we had worked harder, we would be rich today.

(*c*) In an **Unfulfilled Condition,** the **Indicative** is used in the **Principle Clause** with the following verbs, **possum, dēbeō,** and with the **Gerundive** expressing **Obligation.**

e.g. Sī rediissent, servārī **potuērunt.**
If they had returned, they could have been saved.
Sī hōc fēcisset, damnandus **fuit.**
If he had done this, he would have had to be condemned.

136. *Alleged Reason and Qui Causal*

(*a*) In Latin **quod** is used with the **Subjunctive** to indicate that the reason is **alleged** or **supposed** and not a **definite** fact, shown in English by such phrases as, *on the grounds that, for having, because as they said.*

e.g. In vincula cōniectus est **quod** patriam **prōdidisset.**

He was thrown into prison ⎰ *on the grounds that he had betrayed his native land.*
for having betrayed his native land.
because, as they said, he had betrayed his native land.

N.B. Nōn quod with the **Subjunctive . . . sed quia** with the **Indicative** means *not because* (alleged reason) . . . *but because* (true reason).

e.g. Tē culpō **nōn quod** stultus **sīs,** sed quia īgnāvus **es.**
I blame you not because you are foolish, but because you are lazy.

N.B. In an **Alleged Reason sē** is used to refer to the **Subject** of the **Main Verb** if **Third Person.**

e.g. Is eques mē ōderat quod **sibi** nocuissem.
That knight hated me because, as he maintained, I had injured him.

(*b*) In Latin **quī** can be used with the **Subjunctive** to express **Cause**.

> e.g. Mihi īrāscēbātur **quī** ē castrīs **discessissem.**
> *He was angry with me for leaving the camp.*

137. *Concessive Clauses*

(*a*) In Latin **licet, ut, nē,** are used with the **Subjunctive** to concede a fact for the sake of the argument, shown in English by such phrases as, **granted that, suppose that.**

> e.g. $\begin{Bmatrix} \textbf{Licet} \\ \textbf{Ut} \end{Bmatrix}$ **sit** improbus; ūtilis tamen reīpūblicae est.
> *Granted that he is wicked; yet he is useful to the state.*
> **Nē sit** summum malum dolor, malum certē est.
> *Suppose that pain is not the worst evil, yet surely it is still an evil.*

(*b*) In Latin **quamvīs** with the **Subjunctive** can mean (1) *although* (2) *however* (*much*).

> e.g. **Quamvīs** cōnsul exercituī **praesit,** hostēs nōn vincēs.
> *Although the consul is in command of the army, you will not defeat the enemy.*
> **Quamvīs** dīves **sīs,** tē cōnsulem nōn creābunt.
> *However rich you $\begin{Bmatrix} may\ be \\ are \end{Bmatrix}$, they will not elect you consul.*

(*c*) In Latin **etsī, etiamsī,** *although, even if,* are used under **Conditional** rules.

> e.g. $\begin{Bmatrix} \textbf{Etsī} \\ \textbf{Etiamsī} \end{Bmatrix}$ vēra **dīxisset,** iūdex eī nōn **pepercisset.**
> *Even if* $\Big\}$ *he had told the truth, the judge would not have*
> *Although*   *spared him.*

(*d*) In Latin **quī** with the **Subjunctive** is occasionally used to introduce a **Concessive Clause. Tamen** is often present in the Principal Clause.

> e.g. Ego **quī** idem **peccāverim,** tē **tamen** culpō.
> *Although I have committed the same sin myself, yet I blame you.*

138. *Temporal Clauses*

(*a*) **Cum,** *when,* takes the **Indicative** if it expresses **Pure Time** only, and there is no suggestion of **Reason** or **Cause** which would require the Subjunctive. *When* means *at the time when,* and the Subjects of the two clauses are often different and contrasted.

>   e.g. **Cum** nōs Londīniī **erāmus,** tū Rōmae manēbās.
>   *When we were in London, you were staying in Rome.*

(*b*) **Cum,** *when,* takes the **Indicative** if it contains the **Principal** thought of the sentence, i.e. is equivalent to *and then.*

>   e.g. Ad focum sedēbāmus **cum** arāneam **animadvertimus.**
>   *We were sitting at the hearth when we noticed the spider.*

(*c*) In Latin **dummodo** is used with the **Subjunctive,** negative **nē,** to mean, *provided that, if only.*

>   e.g. Dīves fīēs **dummodo** lēgēs **nē violēs.**
>   *You will become rich, provided you do not break the laws.*

139. *Uses of Quin*

(*a*) In Latin **quīn** is used for **quī (Generic) non** after a **Negative, Virtually Negative** or **Interrogative Principal Clause.**

>   e.g. $\left\{\begin{array}{l}\text{Nēmō}\\\text{Quis}\\\text{Vix quisquam}\end{array}\right\}$ est **quīn** linguam Latīnam **amet.**
>
> $\left.\begin{array}{l}\textit{There is no one}\\\textit{Who is there}\\\textit{There is scarcely anyone}\end{array}\right\}$ *who does not like Latin.*

(*b*) In Latin such Verbs as **impediō,** *hinder,* **dēterreō,** *deter,* **recūsō,** *refuse,* if **Negative,** may be followed by **quīn** or **quōminus** with the **Subjunctive.**

>   e.g. Nōn recūsābat **quīn** sententiam **dīceret.**
>   *He did not refuse to give his opinion.*
>   Eum nōn dēterrēbimus **quōminus** Rōmā **discēdat.**
>   *We shall not deter him from leaving Rome.*

N.B. (i) These Verbs if **Positive** take **nē** or **quōminus.**

e.g. Eum dēterrēbimus $\begin{Bmatrix} \textbf{nē} \\ \textbf{quōminus} \end{Bmatrix}$ Rōmā **discēdat.**

We shall deter him from leaving Rome.

(ii) Quōminus is also found in the idiomatic phrase, **per mē stābat quōminus. . . .** *It was my fault that . . . not.*

e.g. **Per mē stābat quōminus** speculatōrēs **caperentur.**
It was my fault that the spies were not captured.

(*c*) In Latin **quīn** with the **Subjunctive** follows such phrases as:

facere nōn possum quīn	*I cannot help —ing*
haud multum abest quīn	*be within an ace of*
nihil praetermittō quīn	*I leave no stone unturned to*
fierī nōn potest quīn	*it must be that*

e.g. Facere nōn poterant **quīn rīdērent.**
They could not help laughing.
Haud multum āfuit **quīn** arx **caperētur.**
The citadel was within an ace of being captured.

Note that this idiom is always used **Impersonally,** as is the following one:

Fierī nōn potest **quīn mentiantur.**
They must be lying.

140. *Unfulfilled Past Conditions in Reported Speech*
(*a*) **In Indirect Statement**
The **sī** clause remains in the **Subjunctive,** the **Principal Clause** now becomes an **Indirect Statement** with its **Infinitive** in the form **-ūrum fuisse.**

e.g. DIRECT
Sī hōc scīvissēmus, vēnissēmus.
If we had known this, we would have come.
INDIRECT
Dīximus nōs, sī hōc scīvissēmus, **ventūrōs fuisse.**
We said that we would have come if we had known this.

(b) **In Indirect Question**

The **sī** clause remains in the **Subjunctive**, the **Principal Clause** now becomes an **Indirect Question** with its **Verb** in the form **-ūrus fuerim.**

> e.g. DIRECT
>
> Sī hōc scīvissēmus, vēnissēmus.
> *If we had known this, we would have come.*
>
> INDIRECT
>
> Mīrābāmur num **ventūrī fuerimus,** sī hōc scīvissēmus.
> *We wondered whether we would have come if we had known this.*

N.B. The Verb is also used in the form **-ūrus fuerim** after **Verbs of Doubting** and **Result Clauses.**

> e.g. Haud dubium est quīn nōs **adiūtūrus fuerit** sī rogātus esset.
> *There is no doubt that he would have helped us if he had been asked.*
>
> Adeō īrāscēbātur ut nōs **ictūrus fuerit** nisi discessissēmus.
> *He was so angry that he would have struck us, had we not left.*

141. PRINCIPAL PARTS OF COMMON IRREGULAR VERBS*

abdō -ĕre, **abdidī, abditum,** *put aside, hide*
abiciō -ĕre, **abiēcī, abiectum,** *throw away*
abigō -ĕre, **abēgī, abāctum,** *drive away*
abripiō -ĕre, **abripuī, abreptum,** *tear away*
accendō -ĕre, **accendī, accēnsum,** *set on fire*
accidō -ĕre, **accidī, ——,** *happen*
accīdō -ere, **accīdī, accīsum,** *cut*
accipiō -ĕre, **accēpī, acceptum,** receive
accumbō -ĕre, **accubuī, accubitum,** *lie down, lie at table*
accurrō -ĕre, **accurrī, accursum,** *run to*
addō -ĕre, **addidī, additum,** *add*
adimō -ĕre, **adēmī, ademptum,** *take away*
adipīscor -ī, **adeptus sum,** *obtain*
adiuvō -āre, **adiūvī, adiūtum,** *help*

* Common compounds of fero and eo are to be found on pages 38 and 40.

adorior -īrī, **adortus sum**, *attack*

afflīgō -ĕre, **afflīxī, afflīctum**, *damage, strike against*

aggredior -ī, **aggressus sum**, *attack*

agnōscō -ĕre, **agnōvī, agnitum**, *recognise*

agō -ĕre, **ēgī, āctum**, *do, drive*

alō -ĕre, **aluī, altum** *or* **alitum**, *nourish, rear*

amplector -ī, **amplexus sum**, *embrace*

aperiō -īre, **aperuī, apertum**, *open*

arcessō -ĕre, **arcessīvī, arcessītum**, *send for, fetch*

ārdeō -ēre, **ārsī, ārsum**, *be on fire*

arripiō -ĕre, **arripuī, arreptum**, *snatch*

ascendō -ĕre, **ascendī, ascēnsum**, *climb up*

aspiciō -ĕre, **aspexī, aspectum**, *look at*

attingō -ĕre, **attigī, attāctum**, *touch, reach*

augeō -ēre, **auxī, auctum**, *increase*

bibō -ĕre, **bibī,** ——, *drink*

cadō -ĕre, **cecidī, cāsum**, *fall*

caedō -ĕre, **cecīdī, caesum**, *cut*

canō -ĕre, **cecinī, cantum**, *sing*

capiō -ĕre, **cēpī, captum**, *take*

carpō -ĕre, **carpsī, carptum**, *pluck*

caveō -ēre, **cāvī, cautum**, *beware*

cēdō -ĕre, **cessī, cessum**, *go, yield*

cēnseō -ēre, **cēnsuī, cēnsum**, *think, propose*

cernō -ĕre, **crēvī, crētum**, *perceive*

cingō -ĕre, **cinxī, cinctum**, *surround*

circumdō -ăre, **circumdedī, circumdatum**, *put around, besiege*

circumstō -āre, **circumstetī,** ——, *stand around*

claudō -ĕre, **clausī, clausum**, *close, shut*

cognōscō -ĕre, **cognōvī, cognitum**, *get to know, learn*

cōgō -ĕre, **coēgī, coāctum**, *force, gather together*

colligō -ĕre, **collēgī, collēctum**, *collect*

colō -ĕre, **coluī, cultum**, *cultivate, inhabit, worship*

compellō -ĕre, **compulī, compulsum**, *force together*

comperiō -īre, **comperī, compertum**, *ascertain*

complector -ī, **complexus sum**, *embrace*

compleō -ēre, **complēvī, complētum,** *fill up*
comprimō -ĕre, **compressī, compressum,** *check, restrain*
concidō -ĕre, **concidī, ——,** *fall down*
concīdō -ĕre, **concīdī, concīsum,** *cut down*
condō -ĕre, **condidī, conditum,** *found, store, bury*
cōnficiō -ĕre, **cōnfēcī, cōnfectum,** *finish, complete*
cōnfiteor -ērī, **cōnfessus sum,** *confess*
coniciō -ĕre, **coniēcī, coniectum,** *throw together*
cōnsīdō -ĕre, **cōnsēdī, cōnsessum,** *sit down, take up position, encamp*
cōnsistō -ĕre, **cōnstitī, ——,** *halt*
cōnspiciō -ĕre, **cōnspexī, cōnspectum,** *catch sight of*
cōnstituō -ĕre, **cōnstituī, cōnstitūtum,** *decide, position*
cōnsulō -ĕre, **cōnsuluī, cōnsultum,** *consult*
contemnō -ĕre, **contempsī, contemptum,** *despise*
contendō -ĕre, **contendī, contentum,** *strive, hasten*
contingō -ĕre, **contigī, contāctum,** *touch*
coquō -ĕre, **coxī, coctum,** *cook*
corripiō -ĕre, **corripuī, correptum,** *seize*
crēdō -ĕre, **crēdidī, crēditum,** *believe*
crēscō -ĕre, **crēvī, crētum,** *grow*
cubō -āre, **cubuī, cubitum,** *lie down*
cupiō -ĕre, **cupīvī, cupītum,** *desire*
currō -ĕre, **cucurrī, cursum,** *run*
dēcernō -ĕre, **dēcrēvī, dēcrētum,** *decide, decree*
dēcipio -ĕre, **dēcēpī, dēceptum,** *deceive*
dēdō -ĕre, **dēdidī, dēditum,** *surrender*
dēfendō -ĕre, **dēfendī, dēfēnsum,** *defend*
dēficiō -ĕre, **dēfēcī, dēfectum,** *revolt, fail*
dēiciō -ĕre, **dēiēcī, dēiectum,** *throw down*
dēleō -ēre, **dēlēvī, dēlētum,** *destroy*
dēligō -ĕre, **dēlēgī, dēlectum,** *choose*
dēpellō -ĕre, **dēpulī, dēpulsum,** *drive away*
dēsiliō -īre, **dēsiluī, dēsultum,** *leap down*
dēsinō -ĕre, **dēsiī, dēsitum,** *cease*
dēsistō -ĕre, **dēstitī, ——,** *desist*
dēspiciō -ĕre, **dēspexī, dēspectum,** *despise, look down upon*

dētineō -ēre, **dētinuī, dētentum,** *keep back*
dīcō -ĕre, **dīxī, dictum,** *say*
dīligō -ĕre, **dīlēxī, dīlēctum,** *love*
dīmicō (l), *fight*
dirimō -ĕre, **dirēmī, dirēmptum,** *separate*
dīripiō -ĕre, **dīripuī, dīreptum,** *plunder*
discō -ĕre, **didicī, ——,** *learn*
dīvidō -ĕre, **dīvīsī, dīvīsum,** *divide*
dō -dăre, **dedī, datum,** *give*
doceō -ēre, **docuī, doctum,** *teach*
domō -āre, **domuī, domitum,** *tame*
dūcō -ĕre, **dūxī, ductum,** *lead*
edō -ĕre, **ēdī, ēsum,** *eat*
ēdō -ĕre, **ēdidī, ēditum,** *give out, cause*
efficiō -ĕre, **effēcī, effectum,** *contrive*
egeō -ēre, **eguī, ——,** *need*
ēgredior -ī, **ēgressus sum,** *go out*
ēligō -ĕre, **ēlēgī, ēlēctum,** *choose*
emō -ĕre, **ēmī, ēmptum,** *buy*
ēripiō -ĕre, **ēripuī, ēreptum,** *tear away, rescue*
ēvādō -ĕre, **ēvāsī, ēvāsum,** *go out, escape*
excipiō -ĕre, **excēpī, exceptum,** *catch up, snatch*
exclūdō -ĕre, **exclūsī, exclūsum,** *shut out*
expellō -ĕre, **expulī, expulsum,** *drive out*
experior -īrī, **expertus sum,** *test, risk*
exuō -ĕre, **exuī, exūtum,** *strip*
faciō -ĕre, **fēcī, factum,** *do, make*
fallō -ĕre, **fefellī, falsum,** *deceive*
for -fārī, **fātus sum,** *say, speak*
fateor -ērī, **fassus sum,** *confess*
faveō -ēre, **fāvī, fautum,** *favour*
feriō -īre, **percussī, ictum,** *strike*
fīdō -ĕre, **fīsus sum,** *trust*
fīgō -ĕre, **fīxī, fīxum,** *fix*
findō -ĕre, **fidī, fissum,** *split*
fingō -ĕre, **finxī, fictum,** *feign, invent*

flectō -ĕre, **flexī, flexum,** *bend*
fleō -ēre, **flēvī, flētum,** *weep*
flōreō -ēre, **flōruī,** ——, *flourish*
fluō -ĕre, **flūxī,** ——, *flow*
fodiō -ĕre, **fōdī, fossum,** *dig*
foveō -ēre, **fōvī, fōtum,** *cherish*
frangō -ĕre, **frēgī, frāctum,** *break*
fruor -ī, **frūctus** *or* **fruitus sum,** *enjoy*
fugiō -ĕre, **fūgī, fugitum,** *flee*
fulgeō -ēre, **fulsī,** ——, *gleam*
fundō -ĕre, **fūdī, fūsum,** *pour, rout*
fungor -ī, **fūnctus sum,** *perform*
furō -ĕre, ——, *rage*
gaudeō -ēre, **gāvīsus sum,** *rejoice*
gemō -ĕre, **gemuī, gemitum,** *groan*
gerō -ĕre, **gessī, gestum,** *carry, manage*
gignō -ĕre, **genuī, genitum,** *beget, produce*
haereō -ēre, **haesī, haesum,** *stick*
haurio -īre, **hausī, haustum,** *drain*
hortor -ārī, **hortātus sum,** *encourage*
iaceō -ēre, **iacuī,** ——, *lie (down)*
iaciō -ĕre, **iēcī, iactum,** *throw*
īgnōscō -ĕre, **īgnōvī, īgnōtum,** *pardon*
immineō -ēre, ——, ——, *overhang, threaten*
impellō -ĕre, **impulī, impulsum,** *drive on*
impendeō -ēre, ——, ——, *overhang, threaten*
incendō -ĕre, **incendī, incēnsum,** *burn*
incidō -ĕre, **incidī, incāsum,** *fall into*
incīdō -ĕre, **incīdī, incīsum,** *cut into*
incipiō -ĕre, **coepī, coeptum,** *begin*
inclūdō -ĕre, **inclūsī, inclūsum,** *shut in*
incumbō -ĕre, **incubuī, incubitum,** *lie on*
indulgeō -ēre, **indulsī, indultum,** *gratify*
induō -ĕre, **induī, indūtum,** *put on*
īnflīgō -ĕre, **īnflīxī, īnflīctum,** *strike against*
ingredior -ī, **ingressus sum,** *enter*

inicio -ĕre, **iniēcī, iniectum,** *throw into*
intellego -ĕre, **intellēxī, intellēctum,** *understand*
interclūdō -ĕre, **interclūsī, interclūsum,** *cut off*
interficiō -ĕre, **interfēcī, interfectum,** *kill*
īrāscor -ī, **īrātus sum,** *be angry*
iubeō -ēre, **iussī, iussum,** *order*
iungō -ĕre, **iūnxī, iūnctum,** *join*
iuvō -āre, **iūvī, iūtum,** *help*
lābor -ī, **lāpsus sum,** *slip, glide*
lacessō -ĕre, **lacessīvī, lacessītum,** *provoke*
laedō -ĕre, **laesī, laesum,** *harm*
lateō -ēre, **latuī, ——,** *lie hidden*

lavō -āre, **lāvī,** $\begin{cases} \textbf{lautum} \\ \textbf{lavātum} \\ \textbf{lōtum} \end{cases}$, *wash*

legō -ĕre, **lēgī, lēctum,** *read, choose*
licet -ēre, **licuit, ——,** *it is allowed*
linquō -ĕre, **līquī, ——,** *leave, abandon*
loquor -ī, **locūtus sum,** *speak*
lūdō -ĕre, **lūsī, lūsum,** *play*
lūgeō -ēre, **lūxī, ——,** *mourn*
mālō -mālle, **māluī, ——,** *prefer*
maneō -ēre, **mānsī, mānsum,** *stay*
meminī, meminisse, ——, *remember*
mentior -īrī, **mentītus sum,** *tell a lie*
mergō -ĕre, **mersī, mersum,** *sink*
mētior -īrī, **mēnsus sum,** *measure*
metuō -ĕre, **metuī, ——,** *fear*
minuō -ĕre, **minuī, minūtum,** *lessen, diminish*
misceō -ēre, **miscuī, mixtum,** *mix*
misereor -ērī, **miseritus sum,** *pity*
miseret -ēre, **miseruit, ——,** *pity*
mittō -ĕre, **mīsī, missum,** *send*
mordeō -ēre, **momordī, morsum,** *bite*
morior -ī, **mortuus sum,** *die*
moveō -ēre, **mōvī, mōtum,** *move*

nanciscor -ī, **nānctus** *or* **nactus sum,** *obtain, find*
nāscor -ī, **nātus sum,** *be born*
neglegō -ěre, **neglēxī, neglēctum,** *neglect*
niteo -ēre, **nituī,** ——, *shine*
nītor -ī, **nīsus** *or* **nīxus sum,** *lean, strive*
noceō -ēre, **nocuī, nocitum,** *harm*
nōlō -nōlle, **nōluī,** ——, *be unwilling*
nōscō -ěre, **nōvī, nōtum,** *get to know*
nūbō -ěre, **nūpsī, nūptum,** *marry*
obiciō -ěre, **obiēcī, obiectum,** *throw in the way of*
oblīvīscor -ī, **oblītus sum,** *forget*
obsideō -ēre, **obsēdī, obsessum,** *besiege*
obsistō -ěre, **obstitī,** ——, *stand in the way, resist*
obtineō -ēre, **obtinuī, obtentum,** *occupy, maintain*
occidō -ěre, **occidī, occāsum,** *fall*
occīdō -ěre, **occīdī, occīsum,** *kill*
occurrō -ěre, **occurrī, occursum,** *meet*
ōdī –ōdisse, ——, *hate*
omittō -ěre, **omīsī, omissum,** *leave out*
operiō -īre, **operuī, opertum,** *cover*
oportet -ēre, **oportuit,** ——, *ought*
opprimō -ěre, **oppressī, oppressum,** *crush*
ōrdior -īrī, **ōrsus sum,** *begin*
orior -īrī, **ortus sum,** *arise*
ostendō -ěre, **ostendī, ostentum,** *show*
pacīscor -ī, **pactus sum,** *make an agreement*
paenitet -ēre, **paenituit,** *repent of*
pandō -ěre, **pandī, passum,** *spread out*
pangō -ěre, **pepigī** *or* **pēgī, pāctum,** *fasten*
parcō -ěre, **pepercī, parsum,** *spare*
pāreō -ēre, **pāruī, obtemperātum,** *obey*
pariō -ěre, **peperī, partum** *or* **paritum,** *bring forth young, produce*
pāscō -ěre, **pāvī, pāstum,** *feed*
patefaciō -ěre, **patefēcī, patefactum,** *open*
pateō -ēre, **patuī,** ——, *be open*
patior -ī, **passus sum,** *suffer, allow*

paveō -ēre, **pāvī**, ——, *fear*
pellō -ĕre, **pepulī, pulsum**, *push, drive*
pendeō -ēre, **pependī**, ——, *hang*
pendō -ĕre, **pependī, pēnsum**, *weigh*
percellō -ĕre, **perculī, perculsum**, *strike*
percutiō -ĕre, **percussī, percussum**, *strike*
perdō -ĕre, **perdidī, perditum**, *destroy*
perficiō -ĕre, **perfēcī, perfectum**, *complete*
pergō -ĕre, **perrēxī, perrēctum**, *proceed*
perpetior -ī, **perpessus sum**, *endure*
perspiciō -ĕre, **perspexī, perspectum**, *observe*
pertineō -ēre, **pertinuī**, ——, *reach to, concern*
petō -ĕre, **petīvī, petītum**, *seek, make for, attack*
piget -ēre, **piguit**, ——, *it vexes*
plangō -ĕre, **planxī, planctum**, *beat, bewail*
pōnō -ĕre, **posuī, positum**, *place*
poscō -ĕre, **poposcī**, ——, *demand*
potior -īrī, **potītus sum**, *gain control of*
pōtō -āre, **pōtāvī, pōtātum** *or* **pōtum**, *drink*
praeficiō -ĕre, **praefēcī, praefectum**, *put in command of*
praestō -āre, **praestitī, praestatum**, *stand out, excel*
prehendō -ĕre, **prehendī, prehēnsum**, *seize*
premō -ĕre, **pressī, pressum**, *press*
prōdō -ĕre, **prōdidī, prōditum**, *betray*
proficīscor -ī, **profectus sum**, *set out*
prōgredior -ī, **prōgressus sum**, *advance*
prohibeō -ēre, **prohibuī, prohibitum**, *prevent*
prōiciō -ĕre, **prōiēcī, prōiectum**, *throw forward*
prōpellō -ĕre, **prōpulī, prōpulsum**, *drive forward*
prōspiciō -ĕre, **prōspexī, prōspectum**, *look forward*
pudet -ēre, **puduit**, ——, *be ashamed*
quaerō -ĕre, **quaesīvī, quaesītum**, *seek*
queror -ī, **questus sum**, *complain*
quiēscō -ĕre, **quiēvī, quiētum**, *rest*
rādō -ĕre, **rāsī, rāsum**, *scrape*
rapiō -ĕre, **rapuī, raptum**, *seize*

recipiō -ĕre, **recēpī, receptum,** *recover, welcome*
reddō -ĕre, **reddidī, redditum,** *give back*
redigō -ĕre, **redēgī, redāctum,** *drive back*
redimō -ĕre, **redēmī, redēmptum,** *buy back, ransom*
regredior -ī, **regressus sum,** *retreat*
relinquō -ĕre, **relīquī, relictum,** *leave behind*
reor -ērī, **ratus sum,** *think*
repellō -ĕre, **reppulī, repulsum,** *drive back*
reperiō -īre, **repperī, repertum,** *find out*
rēpō -ĕre, **rēpsī, rēptum,** *creep*
reprimō -ĕre, **repressī, repressum,** *hold back*
resistō -ĕre, **restitī, ——,** *resist*
respiciō -ĕre, **respexī, respectum,** *look back*
respondeō -ēre, **respondī, respōnsum,** *reply*
restituō -ĕre, **restituī, restitūtum,** *restore*
restō -āre, **restitī, ——,** *remain*
retineō -ēre, **retinuī, retentum,** *hold back*
revertor -ī, **revertī, reversum,** *turn back, return*
rīdeō -ēre, **rīsī, rīsum,** *laugh*
rumpō -ĕre, **rūpī, ruptum,** *burst*
ruō -ĕre, **ruī, rutum** *or* **ruitūrus,** *rush, fall*
saliō -īre, **saluī, ——,** *leap*
sanciō -īre, **sānxī, sānctum,** *decree, ratify*
scandō -ĕre, **scandī, scānsum,** *climb*
scindō -ĕre, **scidī, scissum,** *cut*
sciō -īre, **scīvī** *or* **sciī, scītum,** *know*
scrībō -ĕre, **scrīpsī, scriptum,** *write*
sculpō -ĕre, **sculpsī, sculptum,** *carve*
sēcernō -ĕre, **sēcrēvī, sēcrētum,** *set apart*
secō -āre, **secuī, sectum,** *cut*
sedeō -ēre, **sēdī, sessum,** *sit*
sentiō -īre, **sēnsī, sēnsum,** *feel, perceive*
sepeliō -īre, **sepelīvī, sepultum,** *bury*
sequor -ī, **secūtus sum,** *follow*
serō -ĕre, **sēvī, satum,** *sow*
serō -ĕre, **seruī, sertum,** *join*

serpō -ĕre, **serpsī, serptum,** *crawl*

sileō -ēre, **siluī, ——,** *be silent*

sinō -ĕre, **sīvī, situm,** *allow*

sistō -ĕre, **stitī, statum,** *set up*

soleō -ēre, **solitus sum,** *be accustomed to*

solvō -ĕre, **solvī, solūtum,** *loosen*

sonō -āre, **sonuī, sonitum,** *sound*

sortior -īrī, **sortītus sum,** *draw lots*

spargō -ĕre, **sparsī, sparsum,** *scatter*

spernō -ĕre, **sprēvī, sprētum,** *despise*

spondeō -ēre, **spopondī, spōnsum,** *promise, pledge oneself*

statuō -ĕre, **statuī, statūtum,** *decide, set up*

sternō -ĕre, **strāvī, strātum,** *lay low*

stō -āre, **stetī, stātum,** *stand*

strepō -ĕre, **strepuī, strepitum,** *make a noise*

stringō -ĕre, **strinxī, strictum,** *draw (a sword)*

struō -ĕre, **strūxī, strūctum,** *build, erect*

studeō -ēre, **studuī, ——,** *pay attention to, study*

suādeō -ēre, **suāsī, suāsum,** *advise*

subdō -ĕre, **subdidī, subditum,** *put beneath*

subigō -ĕre, **subēgī, subāctum,** *subdue*

succurrō -ĕre, **succurrī, succursum,** *help*

sūmō -ĕre, **sūmpsī, sūmptum,** *take up*

surgō -ĕre, **surrēxī, surrēctum,** *get up*

suscipiō -ĕre, **suscēpī, susceptum,** *undertake*

sustineō -ēre, **sustinuī, sustentum,** *withstand*

taedet -ēre, **taeduit** *or* **pertaesum est,** *it tires*

tangō -ĕre, **tetigī, tāctum,** *touch*

tegō -ĕre, **tēxī, tēctum,** *cover, protect*

tendō -ĕre, **tetendī, tentum** *or* **tēnsum,** *stretch*

teneō -ēre, **tenuī, tentum,** *hold*

terō -ĕre, **trīvī, trītum,** *rub*

texō -ĕre, **texuī, textum,** *weave*

timeō -ēre, **timuī, ——,** *fear*

tollō -ĕre, **sustulī, sublātum,** *lift, raise*

tondeō -ēre, **totondī, tōnsum,** *shear*

tonō -āre, **tonuī, tonitum,** *thunder*
torqueō -ēre, **torsī, tortum,** *twist*
torreō -ēre, **torruī, tostum,** *parch*
trādō -ĕre, **trādidī, trāditum,** *hand over*
trahō -ĕre, **trāxī, tractum,** *drag*
trāiciō -ĕre, **trāiēcī, trāiectum,** *take across*
tremō -ĕre, **tremuī,** ——, *tremble*
tribuō -ĕre, **tribuī, tribūtum,** *assign, distribute*
trūdō -ĕre, **trūsī, trūsum,** *thrust*
tueor -ērī, **tuitus sum,** *look at, protect*
tundō -ĕre, **tutudī,** $\begin{Bmatrix} \textbf{tūnsum} \\ \textbf{tūsum} \end{Bmatrix}$, *beat, bruise*
ulcīscor -ī, **ultus sum,** *avenge*
urgeō -ēre, **ursī,** ——, *urge, press hard*
urō -ĕre, **ussī, ustum,** *burn*
ūtor -ī, **ūsus sum,** *use*
vādō -ĕre, ——, *go, walk*
vehō -ĕre, **vēxī, vectum,** *carry*
vellō -ĕre, **vellī, vulsum,** *pull*
vendō -ĕre, **vendidī, venditum,** *sell*
vēneō -īre, **vēniī,** ——, *be on sale, be sold*
veniō -īre, **vēnī, ventum,** *come*
vertō -ĕre, **vertī, versum,** *turn*
vēscor -ī, ——, *eat, feed on*
vetō -āre, **vetuī, vetitum,** *forbid*
videō -ēre, **vīdī, vīsum,** *see*
vigeō -ēre, **viguī,** ——, *flourish*
vinciō -īre, **vinxī, vinctum,** *bind*
vincō -ĕre, **vīcī, victum,** *conquer*
vīsō -ĕre, **vīsī,** ——, *visit*
vīvō -ĕre, **vīxī, vīctum,** *live*
volō -velle, **voluī,** ——, *be willing, wish*
volvō -ĕre, **volvī, volūtum,** *roll*
voveō -ēre, **vōvī, vōtum,** *vow*

Index of Grammar

Latin Index

REFERENCES ARE TO SECTIONS